The Content Planner

A Complete Guide to Organize and Share Your Ideas Online

Angela Crocker

Self-Counsel Press
(a division of)
International Self-Counsel Press Ltd.
Canada   USA

Self-Counsel Press acknowledges the financial support of the Government of Canada through the Canada Book Fund (CBF) for our publishing activities.

Printed in Canada.

First edition: 2017

Library and Archives Canada Cataloguing in Publication

Crocker, Angela, author

    The content planner : a complete guide to organize and share your ideas online / Angela Crocker.

Issued in print and electronic formats.

ISBN 978-1-77040-277-5 (paperback).—ISBN 978-1-77040-472-4 (epub).—ISBN 978-1-77040-473-1 (kindle)

    1. Business writing. 2. Business planning. 3. Web sites. I. Title.

HF5718.3.C76 2017	808.06'665	C2016-905156-0
		C2016-905157-9

Every effort has been made to obtain permission for quoted material. If there is an omission or error, the author and publisher would be grateful to be so informed.

Self-Counsel Press
(a division of)
International Self-Counsel Press Ltd.

Bellingham, WA   North Vancouver, BC
USA   Canada

Contents

3 Step 2: Know Your Audience

6 Step 5: Make an Editorial Calendar

7 Step 6: Create Your Content

Notice to Readers

Laws are constantly changing. Every effort is made to keep this publication as current as possible. However, the author, the publisher, and the vendor of this book make no representations or warranties regarding the outcome or the use to which the information in this book is put and are not assuming any liability for any claims, losses, or damages arising out of the use of this book. The reader should not rely on the author or the publisher of this book for any professional advice. Please be sure that you have the most recent edition.

Dedication

For Paul, Sean, Brian, and Michael who make all things possible, and for Yvonne and Marie who watch over all I do.

Acknowledgments

I am blessed with an extraordinary tribe.

Kimberly Plumley and Peggy Richardson keep me grounded and laughing.

Felice Bisby, Samantha Brulotte, Vandhana Misri, and Shelley Neill exemplify fortitude and grace.

Ann Douglas, Karen Lehtovaara Bannister, Lori Bamber, Danielle Christopher, Lindsay Dianne, and Nicole Breit define me as a writer.

Linda L. Richards shares her wisdom in the turmoil of real life.

Bosco Anthony, Karine Bengualid, Chris Burdge, Nicole Christen, Rebecca Coleman, Elaine Tan Comeau, Rob Cottingham, Karley Cunningham, Steve Dotto, Kelly Farrell, Jason Hall, Bruce Hoffman, Katharine Holmes, Paul Holmes, Tara Hunt, Cadi Jordan, Becky Knight, Walter Lanz, Eric Lotze, Vicki McLeod, Christopher Ninkovich, Suzanne Norman, George Plumley, Alexandra Samuel, Sean Smith, Katy Takaoka, Emily Sara Taylor, and Mairi Welman inspire my research with their work.

A thousand thanks to my tribe, including those not mentioned here, for your caring, honest support.

Introduction

Welcome to *The Content Planner*, your guide to organize and share your ideas online. I'm Angela Crocker. I'm a writer, a teacher, and an information organizer with more than 20 years' experience in business communication. I want you to be successful with your content. Together, we'll establish processes that make good use of your time, create shareable content, and benefit your business.

I encourage everyone to create content about topics they love. The best content is created by people who are passionate about their interests. Share your knowledge and your enthusiasm on whatever subject is important to you. There is personal satisfaction and business value in well-written, well-produced content. Elevate your content creation game. *The Content Planner* is designed to show you steps to become a content superstar.

1. Who Can Use *The Content Planner*?

The Content Planner is for anyone who publishes online. You might own an established business or be starting a new entrepreneurial venture. Maybe you're a creative entrepreneur — a writer, an artist, a musician — wanting to raise your profile and share your work with a wider audience. Or, perhaps, you aspire to share the things you love to establish yourself as an influencer. Whether you work alone, as part of small team, or within the communications department of a larger organization, you'll be able to make the most of limited content marketing time and leverage opportunities to generate sales and reap non-monetary benefits. Whatever your role and situation, this book will help you get your ideas online efficiently and effectively.

Not every business will enhance its success with content sharing. For example, the neighborhood store. The location and long hours are convenient for customers who need to stop by for milk or a chocolate bar. They are just going to drop by without checking a website or podcast first. The corner store's customer arrives knowing what he or she wants and is willing to pay a premium price for the convenience. In this case, the business owner would have limited reason to create a content plan.

In today's market, the convenience store example is the exception. Most business owners should invest time and energy in a content plan. Let's explore some of the most common reasons.

2. Where Can I Use *The Content Planner*?

Online publishing can take many forms. You might write for a website or blog. Perhaps, you're in charge of an email newsletter or, maybe, you produce a podcast or YouTube video series. You can use *The Content Planner* to map out broad themes to share through social media tools such as Facebook, Instagram, or LinkedIn. Together, we're going to gather your ideas and make a plan to publish your content regularly and with purpose. Before we do that, we'll begin by connecting your content to your objectives.

3. How *The Content Planner* Works

Savvy business owners know the importance of publishing frequent, unique content, yet often struggle to take action. Some are overwhelmed at the prospect of brainstorming topics. Others find it a challenge to write, photograph, or record their content. Add to that the trend towards live video and a shy content creator may shut down completely. Still others are muddled by the mechanics of how to use a Wordpress dashboard, the Facebook interface, or an email template. Even folks who accomplish this much are sometimes unable to organize their ideas into a viable publishing schedule so end up publishing nothing. If you struggle with any of these challenges, this book can help you.

The Content Planner walks you through seven steps to success:

Step 1: Determine your purpose.

Step 2: Know your audience.

Step 3: Pick a place to publish.

Step 4: Craft your ideas.

Step 5: Make an editorial calendar.

Step 6: Create your content.

Step 7: Share, monitor, and evaluate.

You'll find an overview of these steps in Chapter 1: How to Use *The Content Planner*. More detailed information is found in the chapters that follow. There's also a workbook in the appendix to help you capture your ideas and a digital download of it if you want extra copies.

4. Benefits of a Content Plan

Creating content is an investment of time and, sometimes, money. A confirmed return on your investment makes it easy to justify spending the resources. With a content plan, you have the potential to experience a wide range of benefits. The benefits that matter most to you will depend on your business model and goals.

Some content creators see a direct return on their investment in the form of product sales, ticket revenue, appointment bookings, consultations, and other revenue creation activities. New money in your virtual cash register sounds great, right? I agree, but keep in mind that financial return should not be your only objective. There are many valuable indirect benefits to a carefully executed content plan.

Indirect benefits can take many forms. First, consider the human resources perspective. Businesses can save paid working hours by having the team focus on making and then executing the content plan. Dedicated, focused planning time is much more efficient and effective than an ad hoc approach. Don't make your team work on content only when they have time or, worse, during unpaid overtime. Good content cannot be created as a side project. It demands focus and action.

The Content Planner method also allows you to capture brainstorms for future content plans without being distracted from the plan in progress. Content planning time is also an opportunity to include other team members. Perhaps a subject matter expert, the founder of your company, or a worker involved in manufacturing could contribute to your content plan. Drawing on many perspectives within a company makes for more interesting and well-rounded content. It's also an opportunity for collaboration and team building, a terrific indirect benefit.

If you work alone, consider inviting key suppliers, customers, or advocates to contribute to your content plan. By inviting them to participate, you demonstrate how much you value and respect their ideas. You also have the benefit of deepening relationships and, sometimes, unexpected mutually beneficial joint projects come out of the collaboration.

Well-planned content must be consistent with your brand's visual look and style. Consistent use of fonts, colors, and graphics add to your business's credibility. Narrowing your efforts to specific topics also makes for more professional writing, photography, and videography that better represent your brand. Externally, content sharing is a great way to build relationships with customers. You will be able to better serve existing customers and get acquainted with potential customers.

Depending on the nature of your business, you might also receive invitations for teaching opportunities, conference speaking gigs, or guest posts. These will help you reach a new, but similar audience. The benefits can also include more website visitors, opt-in email subscribers, and social media followers. Great content lets you take your ideas and products to the places where your fans want to interact with your brand.

5. What Content Can I Create?

For many, the biggest hurdle is knowing what to write about. *The Content Planner* includes brainstorming strategies, research techniques, and idea organization approaches. You'll learn about types of content to consider and have a range of thought starters to inspire you. You'll capture lots of ideas and then prioritize and schedule the ideas that best support your current business objectives. Any great ideas that don't fit your current plans can be set aside for future use.

The Content Planner provides a structure that focuses your business on the types of content that supports your business objectives. This book includes pages to formalize your plans in a pen on paper workbook (see Appendix). There's also a copy on the download kit, if you prefer to work in bytes rather than ink. By knowing what content to create and when, your content team will be empowered to take timely action to meet those deadlines. So, let's get to work.

The content planning cycle can cover any period of time that works for you or your organization. In some cases, you'll map out each quarter so you know what's coming up. Others will work week-to-week. For the sake of showing an example, I'm using one month as the cycle interval throughout the book.

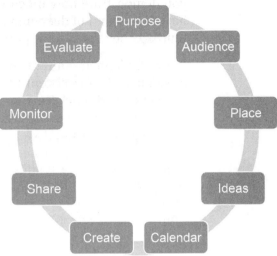

1

How to Use
The Content Planner

The Content Planner is designed to introduce you to a seven-step content creation process. This process is a cycle. Each time you complete the last step, you loop back to the beginning and repeat the process. Depending on how much content you're creating, you may be working on two or more cycles at the same time.

Each content planning step is designed to ensure you've fully addressed all the questions related to your content. There are many things to establish before you create anything, as well as tasks to include after you've published your content.

Resist the urge to skip steps. Each one serves a specific function. If you do them all in sequence, you'll have a strong content plan that includes why, who, where, what, when, and how.

The first time you work through the steps will take longer than subsequent cycles. Future versions of your content plan will refine the work you've done in the past. You'll make modifications to ensure continued success, but you won't have to start from nothing.

If you've been creating content, be sure to refer to any relevant information you already have. If you've done some of the work before reading this, that's great! Use the content planning cycle in this book to improve what you've done in the past.

Collectively, the seven steps give you a repeating framework to create content. Here is an overview of the work ahead.

1. Step 1: Determine Your Purpose

Your first task is to understand why you're creating content and why your audience is interested. If you're clear on the reasons behind your content plan, you'll be more likely to stay committed to the plan and consistently create great content. Very few people can muster the energy to create content without some type of clear motivation.

Every organization and every audience will have a different answer to the question "Why?" Your team might be motivated by marketing or sales objectives. It's also possible you're creating content as a portfolio or to build credibility. Your audience might need help solving a problem or be seeking entertainment. In Step 1, you'll read in detail about common reasons for content creation.

In addition, you'll explore why your audience is interested in your content. Their motivation will likely be different than yours. Think of content creation as a service to support your audience's purpose. The combination of answers that resonates for your audience and supports your business will be the core of your purpose.

2. Step 2: Know Your Audience

Next, it's time to understand your audience. You need to know who will be consuming your content. Ideally, you know your readers, listeners, and viewers personally.

However, those sorts of personalized relationships aren't practical with large groups. If successful, your content may reach an audience of thousands. Maybe more.

To help you know your audience and understand their motivations for consuming your content, I'll include guidelines for creating a persona document to help you visualize your reader, listener, or viewer.

3. Step 3: Pick a Place to Publish

In Step 3, you'll figure out where your content will be published. The location is referred to as your platform. Typically, you'll have a primary platform such as a website, blog, podcast, email newsletter, or video channel. To support your primary platform, you'll also identify secondary locations such as social networks, online communities, and news sites.

This is also your opportunity to decide on what format or formats of content you want to create. Will you be doing text only or sharing text with photographs? You might decide to focus on audio content or video production. Often, a content plan includes a blend of formats that suit your primary and secondary platforms.

4. Step 4: Craft Your Ideas

Exploring ideas is one of my favorite parts of the content planning process. The goal at this stage is to find your ideas. You'll be open to all ideas. You'll identify topics with content potential and seek out the related information.

To find your ideas, you'll use a blend of brainstorming and research techniques. I've included many potential approaches and you'll choose the methods that work for you and your team. I'll also include some thought starters to spark your idea generation in the context of different content styles.

At this stage, all ideas are valid and worthy of consideration. Don't edit yourself in the process. Work to capture as many ideas as possible. The more you have to choose from, the stronger your content plan will be.

5. Step 5: Make an Editorial Calendar

As you build your editorial calendar, you'll start by identifying the strongest ideas from your brainstorming and research. You'll move ahead with these ideas and save any others for future content planning cycles.

Now is also the time to determine who will do this work. I call this group of people the content creation team. If you're from a small organization you may be working alone to complete all the writing, photography, audio recording, and/or videography needed. It's a lot for one person to handle so I encourage you to request access to additional resources. Skilled freelancers can be a great asset to your content creation process. Larger organizations will bring together a team of people to help create the content and support it with copyedits, graphics, uploads, and so on.

Once you know what content you want to create and who's going to create it, you'll focus on your editorial calendar to establish publication dates as well as the pre-publication and post-publication tasks necessary to support your content. This step is complete when you have a working calendar to reference as you create your content. This calendar will help you focus and make clear what content is top priority on a given day.

6. Step 6: Create Your Content

In Step 6, the focus shifts to creating your content. It's time to write the paragraphs, take the pictures, and/or record the video. I've included some advice to help you create web-friendly copy, strong images, and consumable audio-visual content. This is also the time to contemplate legal considerations related to content. I'll make you aware of issues like copyright and model releases. We'll discuss different approaches to the approval process.

Throughout this book, I use content as a collective noun. It includes written text, photographs, illustrations, infographics, audio recordings, and videos. Content also includes formats that combine two or more different types of content like web pages or email newsletters.

For brevity's sake, I'll sometimes emphasize a particular format. Remember that you can still use that information if you're creating content in a different format.

7. Step 7: Share, Monitor, and Evaluate

In Step 7, you begin by sharing your newly published content with your audience through email, social media, and in-person events such as conferences and networking lunches. By sharing your content, you'll help connect your target audience with your work. You'll also devote time to monitoring the response by email and through social media. This is your opportunity to build relationships with audience members through interaction.

Finally, we'll quantify and evaluate your content's success so that you can begin the next cycle of content planning with this information in mind.

8. Appendix: Content Planner Workbook

Throughout the 7 steps you'll see reference to *The Content Planner* workbook in the appendix. The workbook is there to help you capture content-related information, from your purpose statement to brainstorms to your social sharing promotions. Additional copies of the workbook are available in the download kit included with this book.

9. Adapt to Suit You

After many years of teaching content planning, I know there are many different approaches to this process. The steps I describe here are based on my experience and my former students' and clients' experience. This book is an amalgamation of wisdom and success but each successful plan had variations.

You may start out copying my method. However, I want you to feel empowered to adapt the process to your needs so that you get the most out of content planning. Feel free to modify the content planning loop to suit the workflow within your organization. You may change the order of steps or combine them into a single process. Make use of this material so that it works for you.

I also want to encourage you to take imperfect action. I strongly believe that some action is better than no action at all. With each imperfect action, you learn a little bit more about what works and what doesn't. The next time you do that action, you'll improve your approach. Imperfect action is also a remedy for perfectionism. Sometimes good enough is OK and I'd rather see you meet your deadlines than waste tons of time on incremental improvements. Deadlines are important to keep your content plan on track. Use your content resources, especially time, wisely. Delays in your current cycle impact future cycles. Take imperfect action to keep things moving.

Sound good? If you're ready, read on and we'll get started on your content plan. Start with Chapter 2.

Purpose

Evaluate

Audience

Place

Monitor

Ideas

Share

Create

Calendar

2
Step 1:
Determine Your Purpose

Your content must have purpose. Imagine a garden center writing about how a spacecraft docks with the International Space Station. It's hard to see the connection, right? If that garden center writes about how astronauts are using hydroponics to grow plants in microgravity, the content connection becomes clear. Your job in Step 1 is to identify the reasons why you are creating content.

Just as a business has a mission statement, your content plan needs a purpose statement. In it you'll articulate what you're trying to do with the content you create. Your purpose will serve your audience's needs.

A company's current corporate documents can be a great source for your content's purpose. Look at your marketing plan, sales plan, or other documents for inspiration. In terms of content, ask yourself:

- Why are you creating content?

- How can you serve your audience?

- What do you want to achieve with your content?

- What results will satisfy your business needs?

This first step of the cycle helps you explore these questions and gain clarity on the reasons you create content. Do this before you start developing as there's no point in generating content that's not helping you reach your objectives and serve your readers. Once you're clear on your purpose, it's easier to identify content ideas that support your business.

1. Craft a Purpose Statement

A purpose statement is a foundational piece of your content plan. This brief document summarizes your reasons for creating content. Of course, brevity is subjective. Three sentences might be the correct length for one purpose statement, while a full page might suit another. Don't be concerned about the length of your purpose statement, at first. Focus on capturing why you want to create content and what you hope to achieve. You can edit for brevity with each subsequent content planning cycle.

The purpose statement "We strive to create content that will help business owners communicate more effectively," includes what I do, why I create content, and what I hope to achieve. Your purpose statement is for your eyes only. It's not a public document. I share mine in this book only to illustrate the idea. Let's explore potential components of your purpose statement.

2. Why Are You Creating Content?

Most businesses today are fueled by digital promotion and online customer service. Business owners, like you, look to create content to highlight their expertise, differentiate their product, and build relationships with their customers. Influencers — those content creators who curate the world for their custom audience — create content to establish credibility, grow their audience, and add value for their brand partners. Don't be limited by these generalities. Your reasons for creating content should be personalized and specific as you write your purpose statement.

2.1 Content for marketing and promotion

At its simplest, creating content is about marketing and promotion. Content marketing runs concurrent with paid advertising. The content you create complements and enhances advertising opportunities such as display ads, sponsored links, or radio spots, though the content planning method is intended to help you create content, not advertising. Paid advertising is a parallel track.

SAMPLE 1: PURPOSE STATEMENT WORKSHEET

Purpose Statement Worksheet

Check all that apply:

- ☑ Marketing and promotion
- ☐ Differentiate brand
- ☑ Customer service
- ☐ Market research
- ☐ Portfolio

- ☐ Sales
- ☑ Credibility
- ☐ Grow audience
- ☐ Support partners
- ☐ Others: _____

Purpose Statement

We strive to create content that will help business owners communicate more effectively.

SMART goals to support the purpose statement:

1. The content team will conduct a brainstorming session with six team members by March 4.
2. The marketing team will select topics for eight podcast episodes by March 10.
3. The marketing coordinator will conduct keyword research for each podcast topic by March 20.

Notes:

Content created for marketing and promotion is more subtle than paid advertising though, in some respects, they share features. Both are an opportunity to share details on a product or service including price point and where to make a purchase. Plus both content and paid ads follow a brand's style guide in terms of fonts, colors, logo placement, and so on. But content adds powerful layers of storytelling and emotion.

As an example, a cosmetics company will ensure its content is in sync with its paid advertising. The photos will be of high quality and the graphic design will follow the style guide. The content might include —

- fashion trends for the upcoming season,

- tutorials on how to apply dramatic lipstick,

- safety tips to keep mascara bacteria-free,

- ideas for fun selfies to show off makeup looks, or

- celebrity gossip featuring the brand.

Our example cosmetics company will create content that encourages and facilitates interaction with customers. It might use content to explain product features, provide guidance to consumers, or highlight responses to customer feedback. The content becomes a communication tool to inform and influence customers. This more subtle type of content is appropriate and effective for websites, email newsletters, podcasts, videos and, indirectly, social media channels.

For most companies, marketing and promotion make up one part of why they are creating content, but not the whole reason. Read on to explore other reasons you might include in your purpose statement.

2.2 Content to differentiate your brand

Content can be used to differentiate your brand. It's a great way to give your brand personality and highlight the special extras only you can offer. Think about how many brands of jeans you could wear; how many pizza places are near your home; how many realtors serve your neighborhood. There are lots of business categories where content is essential if you want to make your brand stand out from the crowd.

As an example, consider the pizza. There are so many options; a pizza company for everyone's needs.

- Do you order from a big chain or shop locally, supporting an independent restaurant?

- Do you like artisan pizza or just pepperoni?

- Do you need a gluten-free crust or a dairy-free cheese option?

- Do you dine in, or take out, or want delivery?

- Do you have time to wait or need a quick turnaround?

- Do you prefer to order in person, online, or by telephone?

What makes your company unique? Whether you're a soap maker or a franchise owner in a frozen yogurt company, your brand has characteristics that make it stand out. Those characteristics could be about your products, the people in your company, the way you do business, or anything else. Maybe your company has a unique origin story. If it's important to differentiate your company from your competitors, then your content plan should be designed to share what's uniquely you!

2.3 Content for customer service

A wide range of customer service enhancements can be offered through your content plan. If your customers need reminders or support, you can be proactive with your customer service efforts. Not only can you wow them with your excellent customer service but you can save money by reducing staff costs related to a high volume of customer service emails and phone calls.

As an example, a high-end BBQ retailer has lots to offer clients. Here are some examples of great customer service content in action:

- Video on how to season a cast iron grill

- Long weekend "check your propane" reminders

- Compostable serving ideas to skip dishwashing

- BBQ menus with shopping lists and recipes

- Instructions to winterize your BBQ

Adapt this idea as it suits your products. Can your business be proactive with seasonal reminders? What common questions can you answer in advance? How can you enhance a customer's experience with your product? If you can, then the purpose statement for your content plan should express your intent to provide content for customer service.

2.4 Content for market research

Business owners can also create content to support market research. Well-planned content builds a trust relationship between the business and its customers, especially for service-based companies. Over time, you can start asking your readers open-ended questions and a percentage will reply. Similarly, you can occasionally set up a more formal survey and share the link in your content asking your customers to share their experiences, challenges, and wishes.

A parenting coach might do research on a number of topics, such as:

- Inquiring about favorite school break activities
- Gathering aggregate customer demographics
- Considering communication styles related to food allergies
- Researching incidents of bullying
- Offering tips for talking to kids about drugs and alcohol

Through content creation, you also have the opportunity to do less overt research. Google Analytics, Facebook Insights, and other data tracking can be analyzed to test interest in a particular topic. Our example parenting coach might notice a spike in traffic on posts about drugs and alcohol and want to provide additional content to further support his or her community. High readership on a particular topic can also inform the development of a new product offering.

Most likely, research will wax and wane in your content plan. Just as the full moon comes and goes, your business can't be in perpetual research mode. You've got to make some money!

2.5 Content as portfolio

Content plans can also be used to feature the work of a business. A digital portfolio lets viewers see and hear whatever you create. You also have the opportunity to share your process as well as works in progress. Audiences love a glimpse behind the scenes.

This technique is especially helpful for photographers, novelists, musicians, visual artists, and other creative entrepreneurs. Some product-based companies can also create portfolios by creating photographs or videos to showcase their product lines. While your business goal may be to sell concert tickets, books, or prints, your content plan can highlight your work to engage fans. By sharing snippets regularly, customers stay connected to the work between purchases.

As example, let's look at a potter who might create content to share —

- finished pieces of studio work,
- studies leading up to a finished work,
- images from a demonstration at a community event,

- technique steps from raw clay to wheel to kiln,

- a video studio tour inviting readers into the creative space, or

- extreme close-ups of intricate glaze patterns.

By sharing a portfolio, you present an excerpt of your overall body of work. It's not about sharing everything. That would be giving away too much. Instead, share highlights and featured projects. Using your content plan, you can curate what you share to show the depth and breadth of what you offer, without giving away everything for free.

Anytime you share content online, there is the potential that someone else will steal your work and present it as his or her own. If you're emotionally attached to your work, copyright violations can be a painful discovery.

In some cases you can seek compensation or, at least, credit, especially if you have a trademark to protect. More often, the results are not worth your time and energy. Chalk it up to a life experience and move on. Still, you can take steps to make it harder for people to rip you off. Try adding a watermark or digital signature to your images, for example. You can also set up a Google Alert for distinct passages of your writing, and Google can email you if it discovers the wording somewhere.

If sharing your work will enhance your business, then your portfolio becomes a reason you are creating a content plan. Mention it in your purpose statement.

2.6 Content to generate sales

A desire to generate sales is both a legitimate and complex reason for creating content. But pursue this reason carefully. Nothing is more off-putting and brand-damaging than a constant diet of salesy content. That said, it's OK to sell. In fact, some of your readers may be looking for opportunities to buy from you.

So often business owners, especially those with less experience in creating online content, focus solely on selling. They want to see the return on investment (ROI) for every piece of content. Unfortunately, ROI doesn't work quite that linearly. Make sure your purpose statement includes more than just sales goals.

As you create content to sell your product or service, know that you have to give away a certain amount of information for free. Think of it as a sampling program combined with a public relations campaign. I advise people to come from a place of service if they want to create content to generate sales. If you create free content in a well-intentioned way, a percentage of your audience will want to buy the rest from you.

Be sure the free sample is a whole idea that can used fully without an add-on purchase. If you consistently create great content, some of your audience will become true fans who buy one of everything you sell.

Let's say a marketing expert wants to sell an online course. The content will flow through a series of free and paid steps, like this:

1. Small pieces of content shared for free through social media.

2. Invitation to join an email list for exclusive, free tips.

3. Free instant gift with email subscription.

4. Invitation to attend free webinar.

5. Free webinar with great content, including a sales offer.

6. Paid, six-week virtual course.

7. Ongoing free email and social media content.

8. Another sales offer.

9. And so on …

This sequence of free and paid content is part of a sales funnel. Each step of the way, potential customers self-select whether or not to consume the next piece of content. A large group will consume only the free steps. Some will pay for additional content. A small group will consume all the content: These are your super fans.

The content in your sales funnel won't all be sales oriented. (Remember what I wrote earlier about the potential to alienate your audience.) Prevent this problem by incorporating content created for other reasons on your purpose statement.

A successful content plan with sales goals in mind has to include both free and paid content. It's kind of like a romantic relationship: Introduction, first date, going steady, engaged, married. Each step of the way you cultivate your relationship with your audience, and the number of introductions is far greater than the number of marriages.

Many businesses now include list building in the marketing plan. This is a strategy to legally gather email addresses from interested and potential customers. The rules vary by country, but I consider

it best practice to ensure your subscribers opt in. Double opt-in is even better. Only then do you know for sure you have permission to send them content by email.

To ensure your list building efforts are in compliance with local laws, research current requirements. In the United States, look for the Electronic Communications Privacy Act (ECPA) and the related revisions in The USA Patriot Act. In Canada, seek out the *Personal Information Protection and Electronic Documents Act* (PIPEDA) for the private sector and the *Privacy Act* for the public sector.

Don't forget that you must include an unsubscribe link in every message sent. Don't be disappointed if someone unsubscribes. He or she may choose to interact with your content through a social media channel instead, and if he or she is not interested in the content you offer then odds are you are not dealing with your ideal client.

If your purpose statement includes "generate sales," then take time to think about what sort of sales approach will work best in your situation. A soft sell allows you to demonstrate the features of your product or service and provide information to support the buying decision. In contrast, a hard sell pushes your potential customer to make a decision.

A third option is to hand sell which involves customizing the sales approach for each sale. This works best with small volume businesses or high-end businesses catering to the wealthy. You may have experienced hand selling when talking with a jewelry maker at a craft fair or when shopping for a new car.

That's enough about sales for now. Add sales to your purpose statement in the workbook in the appendix if it's right for your content plan.

2.7 Content and credibility

Both businesses and, especially, influencers craft content plans to help establish and maintain their credibility. Through content they demonstrate their knowledge and solidify their reputations as authorities. This can be done by sharing detailed, current information on a topic. Some seek credibility in a broad industry like sports or architecture, while others work to establish deep authority in a specific niche such as women's college basketball or suspension bridge safety. Every piece of content is carefully fact-checked to ensure it enhances credibility.

As an example, a travel influencer with an expertise in tropical vacations might create content like this:

- Surviving a 14-hour flight

- Packing light tips to travel with carry-on only

- Best places to stay for a family of five

- How to barter at the secondhand book market in Adelaide

- Snorkeling adventures on Australia's Gold Coast

- Conservation of nocturnal penguins on Kangaroo Island

The first three examples help establish broad credibility while the last three examples affirm our example travel influencer's deep knowledge of Australia's coast. Your organization might seek broad or niche credibility depending on your industry.

If credibility is why you're creating content, mention it in your purpose statement.

2.8 Content to grow your audience

A content plan can also be used to grow your audience. Are you looking to find more people similar to your current readership? If you sell a product, perhaps you sell locally and now want to expand to a new geographic region. To do so, you can create content to engage people in that new place. Or maybe you have a product for adults and are bringing out a teen version. If that's the case, then you'll want to create content to attract that new demographic.

Similarly, if you run a service-based company you may currently be serving your clients one-on-one. That's great but there are only so many hours in the day. Perhaps you want to use content to attract a wider client base interested in group learning. If you are looking to share your services more widely then to grow your audience may be your goal.

Influencers are almost always looking to grow their audiences. With more people connecting to their content, the influencer can offer clients a bigger audience, and thereby charge more for services. That increase in fees is a business win for the influencer and the larger audience is a win for their clients. Great content makes it a win for the audience.

Whether you sell a product, offer a service, or function as an influencer, the more people in your audience, the more potential readers, listeners, and viewers you can reach. That larger audience has the potential to translate into more customers, too!

If a bigger audience is key to your business success, then be sure to include "grow audience" on your purpose statement.

2.9 Content to support business partners

Through a content plan, you can provide value to your business partners. And, in turn, their content plans can benefit your company. Partners can include retailers, service providers, manufacturers, professional associations, host organizations, or any other with which you do business.

As an example, an office supplies company can support partners both up and down the supply chain by:

- Featuring a literacy program sponsored by a pen manufacturer.
- Reviewing the eco-friendly efforts of a notepad manufacturer.
- Highlighting security products for open office spaces.
- Showing photos from a crafts event at the local mall.
- Offering tips on school supply shopping for parents.
- Creating a bulk-buy quick reference to help shoppers.

In this example, the first three reasons support the office supply company's manufacturers and the last three support retailers. All in the supply chain benefit from the content plan. By featuring partners, or co-creating content, you highlight others' involvement in your work. It's a great way to express appreciation, deepen relationships, and illustrate your willingness to work with like-minded businesses.

If your partners are essential to your success, include them in your purpose statement.

2.10 Don't limit your reasons

The nine reasons outlined are the most common ones found in purpose statements. Use this list as a start and think critically about your business. What are you trying to achieve and why? Once you know, you have information to develop the purpose statement of your content plan.

Your purpose statement will be personalized to your business. The more specific your answer the better it will support your content plan.

3. Be SMART As You Develop Your Purpose and Goals

Let's take a couple minutes to review SMART goals, a common business principle. It applies to content planning and lots of other aspects of business. That's why so many business books talk about it.

SMART is an acronym used as shorthand for a five-step process. SMART stands for:

- Specific

- Measurable

- Achievable

- Realistic

- Time-bound

In content planning, we use SMART goals to ensure we are creating content with purpose. They also help us keep the content plan in sync with overall business objectives. It's normal to have more than one concurrent SMART goal in progress at any given time.

Specific means that your goal is laser-focused on your subject. In content planning especially, a finely honed topic will create a better experience for your audience. Don't write about real estate; instead write about family-friendly, residential properties in suburban Chicago.

Measurable means that you have a way of quantifying your goal. That could mean the number of pieces of content you plan to create or the number of readers, listeners, or viewers you seek. Figure out how you will measure your audience. For a website or blog, you could use Google Analytics. Social networks often provide statistics on the number of people who like or comment on a piece of content. YouTube gives you viewer statistics. An increase in your email newsletter subscribers could also be a unit of measure. To articulate your SMART goal you must know what you want to measure and how you will measure it.

Achievable goals put you in control. Can you take action to bring the goal to fruition? If it's reliant on outside forces then the goal is beyond your control. Furthermore, do you have the skills to achieve your goal? Can you accomplish it to a standard in keeping with your brand? Do you need to bring in extra resources to keep your content plan on track?

Set goals in the realm of possibility. A thousand podcast listeners per episode is only realistic if you have 1,000-plus podcast subscribers, and you have to ask yourself truthfully if all subscribers listen to every episode. Think of this as a reality check for your goal. Also look at your goal more broadly; does it fit in with your other business activities? Content creation is only one part of your overall effort. Maybe it's more realistic to set a lower content goal given your other business tasks.

Time-bound goals are confined by a particular period. You decide whether to evaluate your goal in terms of a number of hours, days, or weeks. Some goals are defined by a deadline: X will happen by date Y. Others are used as motivation to get a goal done. You decide the time constraints around your content goals.

Here are three example SMART goals for content planning. I invite you to use these as templates for your own content planning goals.

1. We will write and publish three new blog posts each week for 12 weeks starting on May 1. Fifteen posts will feature our products, 15 posts will feature customer feedback and 6 posts will highlight our retail partners.

2. We will record one podcast per week for the next six weeks, distribute the recording via iTunes, and promote each episode with a custom graphic on Instagram, Facebook, and Pinterest with a goal of engaging 150 of our 1,000-plus listeners.

3. We will hold a content planning session with all five members of our content team within the next ten days to brainstorm and schedule 24 videos to highlight our services to be produced over the next 12 weeks.

However you define your goals, make sure you create them in keeping with your business objectives. Make note of your goals on the Purpose Statement worksheet in the appendix. What do you want to achieve with your content?

4. Protect Your Purpose Statement

Throughout this chapter, we've worked to formalize your purpose statement. You should now know the reasons you want to create content. This will help you make decisions that support your business.

As you move ahead with your content plan, be proactive to keep it in alignment with your purpose statement. The first step is to write down your purpose statement. There's space to add this detail in the workbook in the appendix. The formality of writing it down ensures that all team members are working with the same purpose in mind.

Share your purpose statement with others in your organization, not just those on the content creation team. This may prevent them from adding distractions to your inbox, in the form of off-purpose ideas. Misunderstandings about why you are creating content run the risk of scope creep. Scope creep is when off-purpose ideas consume content creation resources, usually in small, almost unnoticeable increments.

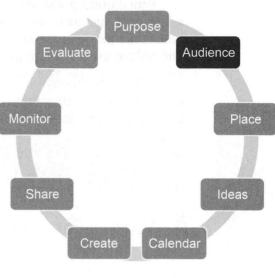

3
Step 2:
Know Your Audience

Who will read, watch, and listen to your content? Your audience and its interaction with your content is at the heart of all your efforts. Whether you call them readers, listeners, or viewers, you need to know them.

Your purpose has to be developed in conjunction with an understanding of your audience. If you don't know who will read your content, how can you find them? Remember it's your job to take content to your audience where they hang out. They won't come looking for you.

In an ideal world, you know your customers personally and have a really great sense of who they are, how they live, and what's important to them. As Emily Sara Taylor said at Digital 2016, "Look at your followers as individuals and cater to their specific needs." Speak to the people who you know are in your audience and come to understand their values, interests, and lifestyle. You know where and how they will consume your content. If you have that kind of relationship with your customers, you are already earning a gold star in content planning.

Your audience may be new or very large. One-on-one conversations with every audience member is an impossible strategy to scale. Do the best you can to connect with as many of them as possible both online and offline. Better understanding begins with that first conversation.

As Bosco Anthony observed at a recent Social Media Camp, "We're all going to start customizing our content to our audience." I'd extend that further to insist you must start creating content customized for your audience. Understand their needs, be part of their story and create content from a place of service. Ideally you know your customers personally but if you don't, get started today. Expand your audience knowledge with the use of a persona.

1. Write a Persona

If you don't know your customers personally, it's common to research and write a persona profile. This tool is designed to help you construct a fictional reader or viewer. It is an amalgamation of all you know about your audience so that you have someone to speak to as you create content. Personas are also known as avatars, ideal customers, target audience, and other, similar terms. In *The Content Planner*, we'll use persona.

Many businesses don't have detailed information about their customers. In many ways they are strangers, no more understood than the person walking towards you in the grocery aisle. There are lots of reasons for this. Your business may be new and working towards developing relationships or it may be established but operating on an enterprise scale with too large an audience to single out a specific user. Most commonly, your business hasn't taken the time to find out. Now's the time!

A persona is a fictional person who represents the qualities and experiences of the people who will read your content. This short description can be shared with all your content contributors so they have a sense of the audience. It will help you make informed decisions about where to connect with your ideal audience.

If you serve more than one audience, as most businesses do, then prepare two or more personas that reflect the range of customers who will consume the content you create. For example, a company like Easy Daysies Magnetic Schedules for Kids would create a persona for each of their target audiences: parents and teachers. Some content will speak to both audiences, but other pieces can be targeted. For example, content about classroom use will focus on the teacher persona while content about bedtime routines will be for parents.

1.1 Persona research

There are many ways to gather information for each persona you write. First, do the research. Some organizations conduct a survey or focus group with existing customers. Others gather anecdotal evidence during interactions with customers in the shop, through social media, at trade-shows, or other events. Some interview staff members about the customers they've met. Sometimes figuring out a persona comes down to an educated guess. That's OK. You'll revisit your persona with each content planning cycle. This gives you the opportunity to amend or update the persona based on the most recent information you have available.

In the sections ahead, we'll talk about the different elements that make up a persona. Look for the Persona Worksheet in the appendix. Fill in details as you read through the rest of this section. If you are serving more than one audience, print an extra copy from the download kit that came with this book. You can also use the worksheet to document your knowledge of a specific person in your audience.

1.2 Demographics

When you think about demographics, start with the basics like age, marital status, number of children, and physical attributes like height and weight, if applicable. Add to that any relevant information you have about location, gender identity, nationality, and genetic heritage. These facts begin to paint a picture of your audience member and can be useful with targeted, paid advertising. Don't stop with demographic facts. You need information to create content that's relevant to your audience.

1.3 Name your persona

Once you've gathered demographic information, give your persona a name. If it is based on a real customer, use a pseudonym for privacy's sake. Don't use a generic John Doe or Jane Smith. Take time to think about it. Does the name evoke a particular cultural heritage? Do Jim Wong, Harry McMaster, and Parminder Sandhu celebrate the same holidays? Do you envision a certain socioeconomic class?

You will spend a lot of time "talking" to your persona, so take the time for a formal introduction.

1.4 Photograph

Next, find a photograph to represent the appearance of your typical customer. Use an anonymous stock photograph, rather than a staff member's photo or a Facebook friend's profile picture. The persona's posture,

SAMPLE 2: PERSONA WORKSHEET

Persona Worksheet

Place
Photo
Here

Demographics:

Age: **42**

Marital Status: **M**

Children: **2**

Height: **n/a**

Weight: **n/a**

Location: **Seattle**

Gender: **female**

Nationality: **USA**

Heritage: **Scottish**

Other:

Name: **Heather Wilson**

Education degree in history, business diploma, ongoing professional dev.	**Economics** earns $50,000+/year, no student debt, mortgage, car loan
Career 10 years' experience in hotel management, now owns event planning company	**Shopping** Likes convenience. Buys groceries online, indulges in coach handbags
Politics egalitarian, active in civic politics, votes Democrat	**Fitness** Struggles to fit workouts in family schedule, enjoys hiking and biking
Religion n/a	**Home** Suburban, single family home near schools, parks, and shopping
Medical In good health. Suffers occasional foot pain from old injury.	**History** Spent a year in Australia at age 22.

grooming, and attire will influence how you perceive them as you create content. Even the setting can add to your persona knowledge, as an urban center is much different than a pastoral setting.

1.5 Education

Beyond the name and photograph, articulate your persona's educational background. Does he or she have a ninth grade education, Red Seal certification in plumbing, or a graduate degree? Look beyond formal academic settings as well. Perhaps your persona holds a third Dan black belt in Taekwondo or is Zentangle certified.

1.6 Career

Next, consider the persona's career development. He or she might be new to the work force with an entry level position. Alternatively, the persona may be a seasoned neurosurgeon working as head of department at a teaching hospital. Your persona's career journey and position give an impression of experience, and how he or she spends time and might consume your content.

1.7 Politics

Next, think about political affiliations. Your persona might be active in politics and a member of a leading political party. In contrast, he or she might steer clear of anything to do with politics and abstain from voting, which gives you a very different sense. Or, perhaps he or she is highly political but new to the country and has to wait to earn the right to vote.

1.8 Religion

Contemplate religion, too. Your persona might be religious, spiritual, or atheist. If he or she identifies with a formal religion, does a Christian, Muslim, Jewish or other formalized faith influence the content you create? Spirituality can mean many things, from angels, runes, and oracles, to guidance through nature. Take time to understand the kind of spirituality that matters to your persona. The atheist in your audience may be a person of pure science or disillusioned with God. Remember those for whom religion and spirituality don't resonate at all.

1.9 Medical

Your persona may be living with a medical condition or may be in good health except for a lingering injury. Perhaps he or she has a permanent physical disability or a weakened immune system. Consider whether your persona is living with an invisible illness like multiple sclerosis or anxiety, or is in good mental and physical health.

1.10 Economics

Also, try to understand your persona's economic position. His or her income might be from casual work, a steady job, a pension, or government support. He or she may be independently wealthy or living off dwindling savings. If struggling to put groceries on the table, or recently bankrupted by medical bills or a natural disaster, his economic position is precarious. If she recently received an inheritance or insurance settlement, her economic position is improving. How do finances influence the content you create?

1.11 Shopping habits

Specify brands your persona purchases, and shopping habits. Shopping at Super Save Groceries indicates a different lifestyle than shopping at farmers' markets and artisanal cheese shops. Busy parents might shop during the day with little ones in tow, or late at night while a parenting partner watches over the kids. Time-strapped professionals may do most of their shopping online for delivery. How do shopping habits influence the content you will create to serve your persona?

1.12 Fitness habits

Your persona's fitness routine, or lack thereof, helps you know him or her better. If active, does he like hiking and biking outdoors or visiting a gym every morning? If she is less active, does she struggle to fit fitness into a busy lifestyle or struggle with an injury that's keeping her still? Make note of your persona's fitness activity on your persona worksheet.

1.13 Home

Where does your persona call home? Individuals who live in a small, urban apartment have different lifestyle choices than those who live in suburban single-family homes or on hobby farms. The location also tells you something about their commuting style. Those who can ride transit have a different experience than those who drive 60 minutes or more each way to work. The number of people sharing the persona's home is also relevant. A single or couple living alone have different pursuits than a family with three children, or four generations sharing a house.

1.14 Personal history

If you've gained the confidence of your customer base, you may know something of their personal history that influences how to communicate with them. A death in the family, a cross-country move, military service, and other life experiences may be part of your persona's history. Take note on your persona worksheet.

2. Compile Your Persona

Once you've considered all the topics, complete the persona worksheet in the appendix. I encourage you to type up your persona for future reference. Rather than type a list of bullet points, craft the information into short paragraphs as though you were introducing your audience member as the honored guest at a banquet. This will give you an even better sense of the whole person.

As you compile your persona, keep in mind that not every category will be fully explored. As you get to know your customer base, you can adapt the persona to more closely reflect the real people who will be consuming your content. Remember that the persona is a helpful construct towards whom to focus your content creation efforts, but it does not replace real relationships with your customers. By formally documenting personas that model your audience, you have a sense of who you're serving and can more effectively identify locations for your platform where your customer hangs out.

3. Contributors

While you're exploring the people who will consume your content, take time to consider who will create your content, too. You'll need talented people to write, photograph, design, audio record, and videotape your ideas. You may be talented at all these formats, but each will take time. Very likely, you're not an expert at everything from writing to graphic design to videography. So, tap into the talent at your office and hire help, if needed, to create your content.

Identify your contributors early so that you can include them in your content planning cycle. Seek contributors who understand your audience and demonstrate experience communicating with people similar to your persona. Tap their expertise as you establish your platform, brainstorm and research content, and so on. A strong content team can reliably and efficiently create the content you need.

3.1 Single contributor

Some businesses will centralize their content creation. If you're a solo entrepreneur, you may be creating all your own content, too. A single contributor does it all: writing, photographing, recording, editing, designing, and uploading. It's a lot of work and in some cases you might be doing the best you can with the skills you have. It's OK to manage on your own and sometimes you have no choice. It's also OK to hire help. If budget allows, add a freelancer to your team to share the workload.

3.2 Staff contributors

If you're part of a bigger team, you may have numerous content contributions from different locations or departments. Get to know your contributors and communicate topics, deadlines, and other details with them as clearly as possible. I'd recommend a shared digital workspace to keep track of everyone's assignments and contributions. Depending on the complexity of your content, your shared digital workspace might be a simple spreadsheet saved on a company server, or a cloud storage solution accessible to all team members. For more complex situations, I recommend using a tool like Slack or Basecamp.

3.3 Editors

Depending on your contributors' skill levels, you may want to add an editor to your content team. For text, you may want two different kinds of editors: a substantive editor who looks at the organization and expression of the big ideas, plus a copyeditor who will review and correct spelling, punctuation, and formatting. In addition, images, audio, and video all have specialist editors available for hire.

3.4 Photographers and videographers

Are you going to take your own photographs or shoot your own video? You may need a photographer to capture the images you require, or an account with a stock photography website. Similarly, hiring a skilled videographer may make sense for your content plan. The key thing is to ensure you have the talent you need to create your content.

3.5 Guest and community contributors

When considering your platform, you may want to invite carefully selected experts from inside and outside your company to contribute content. They may value the opportunity to publish their work, or you might have to pay for their content. It is best practice to vet your guest contributors.

You can also invite your audience members to contribute content. They might share experiences using your product or provide related photos, tips, recipes, or other content. This is an excellent method to engage your community. Their participation deepens the relationship with your brand and adds their circle of influence to your audience. It can also help you identify your true fans.

Again, at this stage, knowing that you can find the guest contributors you need for your platform is all that matters.

> Please don't ask content creators to provide content for free. Too often, a request includes promises of exposure to a new audience. Even if you have 80,000 social media followers, you cannot guarantee your audience will view the content nor can you motivate them to take action to benefit the content creator. Sadly, requests for free content contributions have become common practice. It's not OK to ask for free content. Ever. It is OK to accept free content if it is willingly offered by a friend, supplier, or industry ally.

3.6 Content exchanges

You also have the opportunity to work with a complementary business to share your expertise with one another's audiences. Ideally, you would collaborate with someone who reaches a new group of your ideal customers, and you would, in return, share your audience with them. When you arrange the exchange, be clear about what's expected from each side in terms of editorial style, quality, quantity, and formality. The exchange should be balanced so that both organizations make equal contributions and derive equal value.

3.7 Bylines and credits

Bylines and credits are another consideration when building your content team. Decide if you will give credit. Then, make sure your contributors know they will (or won't) get a byline or credit. Keep in mind some platforms (see Chapter 4 on Step 3) will make it easy to credit contributors while others aren't as straightforward. Some contributors may be unwilling to provide content without a byline.

We'll talk about how to work with contributors when we get to Chapter 7 on Step 6: Create Your Content.

4

Step 3:
Pick a Place to Publish

1. Where to Publish Online

When it comes to publishing online, you have to decide on a digital location. There are many options, from a website to a podcast and much more. As Barbara Pender said at a recent Social Media Camp, "Don't pop on every platform unless you have a strategy." Armed with your purpose in mind and knowledge of your audience, you've got to figure out where you and your customers are going to hang out. Wherever you decide to publish your content is your platform. Where will you publish?

A personalized selection of online locations make up your platform. Typically, you'll have a primary location complemented by two or more supplementary locations. It's most common to publish content in your primary location and then share, or re-publish, as appropriate, the same content on your supplemental locations.

Most likely, your primary location is your company's website, blog, or website with blog. It could also be your YouTube channel, podcast, or email newsletter. Beyond that, there are hundreds of locations to choose from. Your website works in concert with carefully curated news sites, online communities, and social networks. For example, Joshua Malina and Hrishikesh Hirway use a podcast as the primary platform for their successful and entertaining audio series *The West Wing Weekly*. They regularly circulate the podcast to iTunes, Google Play Music, and various other podcasting services. The podcast and related show notes and references are published on their website at www.thewestwingweekly. com. Their platform is further supplemented by a Facebook page and Twitter feeds, locations where their audience spends time interacting with the content online.

Take time to identify your platform locations. Be specific. It is very common (and highly recommended) to use your business's website with a blog as your primary location. The website your own is where you have the most control. In addition, you'll choose several supplemental locations. These might be a podcast or email newsletter, other websites, news sites relevant to your field, plus one or more social networks. Remember, you decide where to share your content.

As you determine your platform, review your desired audience. Who are you trying to reach? The best platform with which to reach small-business owners is very different from the one to reach parents dealing with kindergarten anxiety. We invested time in understanding your audience in Step 2; take time to review your notes now.

When you establish your primary and supplemental platform locations, plan to create content appropriate to those locations. Are you creating text, images, audio, or video? While most websites can display most content types, some are better suited than others. It makes sense to include a video sharing website in your platform if you've got the equipment and the know-how to produce, edit, and upload videos. If movie making is beyond your team's skillset, then creating content in the form of videos isn't a good fit for your platform.

The locations that make up your platform can be adjusted, amended, or deleted at any time. Part of *The Content Planner* cycle involves evaluation. We'll explore how to evaluate your content's success in Chapter 8, Step 7: Share, Monitor, and Evaluate. On your next turn through the planning cycle, you can change your platform, if needed.

Before you abandon a location, consider whether you've given it a fair chance. It takes time to build an audience. It may also take some time to learn to build content ideally suited to a particular location.

Also, keep in mind that the web is an ever-changing landscape. The locations that work in 2017 won't necessarily work as well in 2020.

Over time, you'll learn the locations within your platform that help you achieve your business goals. You'll also be well-prepared to make adjustments to respond to that ever-changing landscape.

2. Choosing a Platform

As mentioned, your platform is made up of a primary location and supplemental or secondary locations. Choose your platform carefully. Changes can be made, but let's start with the most effective platform, based on what you know about your business today. Typically, you'll identify one central place where you will publish content, usually a website, blog, podcast, video channel, or email newsletter. This is your primary platform. In addition, you'll identify one or more secondary locations that support your primary platform.

Depending on your business, you may limit your platform to a single, primary location. This can happen if your topic is a very narrow niche or if your organization has strict rules related to publishing content online. The latter usually happens in heavily regulated industries and in companies working with proprietary intellectual property. A single location platform is also common when the content contributors are new to publishing online. It's OK to start small and grow as you gain experience, confidence, and an audience.

Your content's positive effects will be more robust if you add supplemental locations to your platform. Online communities, news sites, and social networks can support your primary location no matter the platform. Let's explore the various options to help you decide.

2.1 Website

Think of a website as your home on the Internet. As WordPress expert George Plumley suggests, visualize it as your piece of real estate online. In this digital location, you can publish your content, in any digital format. Websites have the advantage that you can design the appearance of the information to match your purpose and your audience's needs. You also have control over things like content management, custom links, and social sharing tools.

There are many tools that can be used to create your website. WordPress, Squarespace, Wix, Weebly, and Drupal can all be edited to create a site that gives the look and feel you want. I admit to a strong preference for Wordpress, but it's a matter of personal taste. If you have an existing site, work with what you've got. If you're starting from scratch, consider hiring a professional web designer to do the initial setup, then take over the content creation and publishing yourself. Think of the behind-the-scenes interface for your site as a content management system.

If you are starting out, establish your website as the primary location in your platform. You'll have the highest degree of control over the look, feel, and content. You're most likely to have copyright ownership of your website's content. In addition, you have control to update each piece of content if you need to amend, revise, or clarify anything in future. Once your website is established it supports any additions to your platform.

2.2 Blog

A blog is a great way to publish content as text, images, audio, or video. Many websites now include a blog and this may be part of your primary location. If not, then consider adding blog functionality or establishing a blog in a secondary location.

The most common primary platform for content creators is a website with a blog. By combining the two options, you have the advantages of a digital home that you control plus blog posts to publish frequent new content. By pooling your content in a flexible space, you can make static information like the biography page or shopping cart easily accessible alongside the dynamic content you share in blog posts.

If you prefer to blog exclusively or want to keep your blog separate from your website, access a blogging service. This allows you to publish content on a standardized platform. Typically, some degree of customization is possible so you can pick a color scheme, add photos, or otherwise brand your blog as your own. Explore tools like Wordpress, Medium, Tumblr, or any one of dozens of other tools. Just remember to blog at a location that is well-supported and demonstrates an active community. Don't waste your time blogging on an outdated platform with few visitors that might be shut down without warning.

2.3 Video

As a content format, video allows you to show and tell your subject. You can infuse your videos with personality and make it easier for your audience to relate to your topic. As the content creator, you establish a channel where fans can subscribe to your content. You may not be HBO but you can have your own broadcast system with the added bonus of two-way digital conversation with your audience.

The most popular platform for video sharing is YouTube. Other video platform options include Vimeo, Flickr, Dailymotion, and Veoh. While it's worth exploring the video service that works best for you, YouTube is the top choice for most content creators.

Beyond a video channel, you might want to explore the potential of livestreaming, where you are sharing real-time events with your digital audience. Viewers have the opportunity to see content they can't attend due to the distances involved, the cost of admission, or the logistics of gaining access to an exclusive event. Livestreaming video tools include Facebook Live, Periscope, Twitch, Busker, and UStream. In addition, don't forget other social video options like Instagram stories and SnapChat.

> Whether producing videos for a video channel or recording a podcast, create a structure for your show. Help viewers and listeners navigate your content. Do this by using consistent opening and closings as well as familiar transitions between segments, including any sponsorship obligations or paid commercials. Further reinforce this in video with consistent use of animations and visuals. Keep to a consistent length, too, whether that be ten minutes or an hour.

2.4 Podcast

In a sense, a podcast is an online radio program delivered via the Internet. Unlike broadcast radio, the audience can listen at any time from any place with an Internet connection. The content is available on demand, making it convenient for your audience to connect with your content when it suits them.

Listeners will seek your content on their preferred podcast service, a directory of podcasts from many different content creators. Your audience will likely use one of the following services:

- iTunes
- Google Play Music
- Soundcloud
- Stitcher
- TuneIn

Listeners can use these apps to listen with their mobile phone, tablet, web browser, and sometimes, through the car stereo.

To share content with your audience, you'll upload your program. You'll use an RSS feed, typically hosted on your website, to send the episode to the directories. Fortunately, there are plug-ins available to streamline the process. I'm most familiar with Blubrry (blubrry.com), the top-rated WordPress plug-in for podcasting.

Initially, you have to authorize your account to prove yours is a legitimate podcast. Then you'll upload each episode, validate the upload and related links, and make the most of available tools to manage your content. The tools range from the ability to add a photo or show notes to social interaction tools and audience ratings. Five stars, anyone?

If you choose to make a podcast part of your platform, you'll be recording and publishing audio content. The audio content you create will be distributed to readers with each new episode.

Steve Dotto of www.dottotech.com is one of my favorite resources for technology advice. In a recent video on his wildly successful YouTube Channel, Steve recommended the following experts for more information about podcasting:

- John Lee Dumas at www.eofire.com/how-to-podcast

- Pat Flynn at www.smartpassiveincome.com/tutorials/start-podcast-pats-complete-step-step-podcasting-tutorial

- Cliff Ravenscraft at www.podcastanswerman.com

After reviewing their content, I concur with Steve's recommendation and share them with you to help to help you succeed with podcasting.

2.5 Email newsletter

Your primary or secondary platform may be an email newsletter. This is especially useful if your purpose statement indicates you want to generate sales or grow your audience. Similar to a magazine, an email newsletter includes a variety of content. Often the information appears as a series of articles with graphics and links. Sometimes an email newsletter is simple type, as you would send to a personal email to a friend.

If you're thinking about publishing an email newsletter, ensure you understand the related privacy legislation. This includes the Electronic Communications Privacy Act (ECPA) in the United States and the *Personal Information Protection and Electronic Documents Act* (PIPEDA) in Canada. If you need a refresher, reread the sidebar in Chapter 2, Section 2.6.

There are a number of services to help you comply, manage your email distribution lists, and publish your content. These include:

- MailChimp

- AWeber

- Constant Contact
- MadMimi

Each of these services records the opt-in details of when and where a subscriber confirmed their interest in your list. They also provide the opportunity to design a template to give your material a professional and consistent appearance. Most importantly, they include functionality to allow your readers to unsubscribe and ensure that you don't accidentally contact them again unless they re-subscribe.

Using a service also increases the chances that your email will be delivered. Rather than send a bulk batch with all your subscribers' email addresses blind copied, the service sends each email individually. Why go to all the trouble of creating content for a newsletter if you can't be sure it's delivered successfully?

MailChimp, AWeber, Constant Contact, MadMimi, and others, all offer robust reports. You'll have statistics to show how many subscribers, new subscribers, and unsubscribes have happened on your list in a given period. The reports will also tell you how many people opened your email and show which links they clicked. Use these statistics to refine email newsletter content in future content planning cycles.

Your email service can help you send downloadable documents and other digital goodies to your subscribers. You can also set up a "drip campaign" to send subscribers a series of emails over a period of time. This can be very helpful as you build relationships with new readers and to provide added value to continuing subscribers.

Cost varies between services. Some are free at first. Others are paid. Usually, there is an incremental cost: the bigger your list, the more you pay. The level of technical support varies, too. Free users have access to online chat while paid users can add human-to-human assistance through phone calls and, sometimes, you're assigned a personalized customer service rep.

If you're ever tempted to worry about the cost of your email subscriber service, consider the cost to send that many subscribers a letter by regular mail. The cost of printing and snail mail postage will quickly overwhelm your budget. Also, most content creators find a way to leverage their email list to earn some money from product sales, advertising sales, or other revenue streams.

2.6 Online communities

Online communities are another good secondary location for your platform. You can find general interest and special interest communities talking about every topic imaginable. A great example is goodreads.com, an online community for book lovers. Participants publish what they're currently reading, what they plan to read, and share reviews of books.

Every topic imaginable is explored in at least one of the thousands of online communities. Some communities have a dozen members while others include thousands of people. I'm almost certain there is a group somewhere for underwater-scarf-knitting-with-wire!

Consult your customer base or review your persona for ideas on online communities of interest to your audience. It's important to seek out communities that are relevant to your audience and have a positive reputation. Use common sense to assess communities and elect to participate where dialogue is meaningful. Plan to contribute on an ongoing basis. By all means share your content but also respond to other people's contributions, answer questions, and offer links to outside resources, even if they are created by someone else.

Most importantly, make sure that you participate in online communities with authenticity. Be true to yourself and your brand. Don't be the person who constantly plugs his or her own work. Do that too often and you'll be removed or, at least, shunned by members of the community with which you're trying to connect. An online community is a place to share information, but you won't always be the author of that information.

2.7 News sites

If your business generates newsworthy news, you may want to add news sites to your platform. Status as a contributing writer or editor will allow you to publish content. Depending on the news site, you may be able to reach the same audience through conventional public relations by sending a press release in hopes of editorial coverage. Or you may be able to be published on the site with a sponsored post.

2.8 Social networks

The biggest category for potential secondary locations in your platform is social networks. Be sure to identify some social networks such as Facebook, Instagram, or LinkedIn as part of your platform. They offer tremendous reach. The biggest social networks in North America include:

- Facebook (1.65 billion users)
- YouTube (1 billion users)
- LinkedIn (414 million users)

- Instagram (400 million users)
- Twitter (316 million users)
- Google+ (300 million users)
- Snapchat (100 million users)

That's a lot of people using social networks. Of course, the number of registered users noted above will be higher than the number of active users in any given week. We've all seen those weird spam accounts and, over time, users abandon one social network in favor of another. Remember MySpace? Ello? Blab? However, with millions of active users, you have the potential to connect with millions of potential customers. That's a lot of prospects!

Please don't restrict yourself to the communities, social networks, and outlets listed above. There are hundreds to choose from. Ask around in your industry. Ask your customers. Figure out where your ideal customer is going to be and then plan to participate. Work to become a helpful, caring voice in that community. Create content to be of service to them. Do not make the mistake of becoming a spammy, self-serving contributor. You'll be banned and harm your reputation.

> Business coach and author Vicki McLeod has encouraging words when it comes to social networks. In her book *#Untrending*, she wrote, "There's a social media platform for you. Find your voice, find your beat, find your platform. Fall in love with it, or at least get a good infatuation going." As you explore social networks, you'll find that Vicki is right.

Once again, as you select social networks to include in your platform, consider where your ideal audience is going to spend time. Will you find them on Facebook and LinkedIn or are they more likely to be Instagram and Snapchat users? Demographics, buying patterns, and other elements of your ideal audience's persona will guide you.

3. Who Owns Your Platform?

Ownership is a big consideration when mapping out your platform locations. The only location you own and control is on your own self-hosted website. Think of it as a piece of digital real estate. This is yet another reason to make your website your primary location in your platform. That said, you can't control where links to your content will be shared. Your content may be circulated by someone with an opposing view or on a spammy site. This is the nature of the Internet.

Don't let content ownership stop you from adding supplemental locations beyond your control. To share content with maximum effect, you need a wide reach. Some of that is beyond your control. There's an element of risk when you share your content online. But there's a greater chance of a larger audience finding and connecting to your ideas.

4. Length and Format

As you consider your platform, take time to consider the length and format of the content you'll be creating. Content can take many forms: text, images, audio, and video. Sometimes the content is short while other times it's lengthy. Sometimes it's meant to last for a long time and other times it's meant to be consumed briefly in a moment of time.

4.1 Text

There's much debate about the ideal length for text. How long is long enough? You'll want enough words to convey your meaning. At the same time, avoid lazy writing filled with unnecessary words to reach a particular word count. Succinct writing takes time and skill. Brevity will make your brand look smarter. Remember Mark Twain's comment, "I didn't have time to write you a short letter, so I wrote you a long one instead."

I recommend you have two lengths for your text. Some articles will be 300 words in length (the current minimum to satisfy search engines that your content is legitimate) while others will be 2,000 words. In a 300-word post, use a factual, journalistic style. Tell the reader the five Ws: who, what, where, when, and why. Ensure the facts are all included for quick reference. In a longer post of 2,000 words, you can add opinions, references, and context.

At any length, remember to write with keywords in mind in order to have your content turn up correctly in search engines. We'll explore keywords fully when we get to Chapter 7, Step 6: Create Your Content.

4.2 Images

Images can take many forms: photographs, graphics, icons, illustrations. Images increase the visibility of your text. The types of images you'll include depend on your skill to create them.

These days everyone is a photographer. I subscribe to professional photographer Manfred Forest's advice that you should use the best camera you have on hand. That might be a fancy digital SLR, but often it's the camera in your mobile phone. Take the best picture you can with the camera you have with you.

Later in this book, we're going to look at a variety of intellectual property considerations including copyright and model release related to images. See Chapter 7, section 7., Legal Considerations.

4.3 Audio

Audio can be a powerful tool to humanize a brand. Hearing an expert speak can solidify your brand as an authority. It's also a great way to gather content for sharing without having to write text. Sure, you could write a script and record someone reading it back, but the real magic happens when the remarks are original and off the cuff. The audio could be of a single person sharing information lecture-style, or it could be a conversation between two or more people. Each person brings a different energy to an audio recording.

As with all forms of content creation, there's a range of audio recording quality. To ensure the most listeners, aim for the highest possible audio quality. We'll talk about different methods to record audio in Chapter 7 on Step 6. Once recorded, publish your audio on your website or as a podcast.

4.4 Video

Video is a wonderful way to tell a visual story. It's like digital show and tell for your ideas and products.

YouTube is the number two search engine behind Google (and it's owned by Google). As such, incorporating some video into your content creation can be great for visibility. You have the option to create your own informal video or work with a videographer to shoot and edit your material. Once recorded, video can be uploaded to YouTube, Vimeo, Facebook video, and other video sharing sites. Many of these sites, particularly YouTube and Vimeo, make it easy for you to embed a video player on your website.

Think also about live video. Tools like Facebook Live and Periscope allow you to broadcast content in real time. Short clips can also be shared live through tools like Instagram Stories and Snapchat. How can your brand create content suitable for live video?

5. Your Platform Plan

At this point, you should have a clear idea of your platform. Write down your primary location as well as your supplemental locations on the platform worksheet. The plan you make today is sufficient. We'll evaluate and make improvements to it in the next content planning cycle. It's time to move on to Chapter 5, Step 4: Craft Your Ideas.

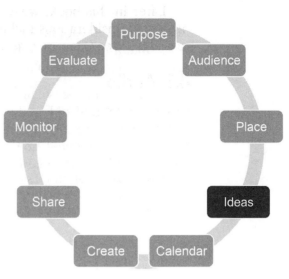

5

Step 4:
Craft Your Ideas

A content plan is of no use without lots of ideas for the content itself. In this step, I share strategies to help you brainstorm bountiful ideas and gather useful research. This is one of my favorite parts of content creation. I hope you enjoy it, too.

I'm including example ideas from one of my projects to spark your thinking. You'll set up a structure to ignite your imagination and you'll be one step closer to creating interesting and engaging content.

1. Focus Your Topic

The content you create has to serve the audience you got to know in Step 2. As Vicki McLeod said, "whatever you're making must solve their problem, relieve their pain or empower their dream." Your ideal reader is consuming your content based on interest in a specific subject. To keep his or her attention, you want to ensure that you focus your topic.

Remember to also refer back to your purpose statement. You've already done the work in Step 1 to understand why you are creating content. Take a moment to refresh your memory. Your purpose statement and topic selection should support one another.

Finding your focus can be a tricky business. Too general a topic will draw a wide audience but only a small percentage will be the people you want to attract. Conversely, too narrow a topic limits the potential size of your audience and the scope for what content you can create. The perfect focus is somewhere in between and it takes a bit of guesswork to find the right scope for your content.

Take for example, a dollhouse manufacturer. What would its focus look like?

- The history of toys including design, manufacture, safety standards, and the socioeconomic culture that surrounds them.

- Manufacture of dollhouses made in the colonial style produced in the United States with natural woods.

- The history of dollhouses including architecture and manufacture with a focus on artisans building dollhouses and related accessories.

In the first example, the focus may be too broad. Certainly, dollhouse enthusiasts will be interested in the design of the houses and accessories. They'll also likely be keen to learn about manufacturing and how to make it themselves. But are dollhouse enthusiasts interested in other types of toys? Probably not. They may not care about safety standards. And they live the culture surrounding dollhouses so they may not need you to give them information about it.

The second example may be too narrow. Dollhouses have a long history in many countries and cultures. They are made from many materials including woods, plastics, and metals. Artisans and factories create dollhouses all over the world, not just in the United States.

The third example is a strong candidate for the ideal focus. Its central focus on artisan work will attract readers interested in handmade dollhouses, rather than those mass-produced in factories. The tie-in with architecture is logical as artisans — both professional and amateur — need guidance to ensure their dollhouse builds are a success. The laws of physics apply!

As you can see in our dollhouse examples, the focus topic is an umbrella for numerous related subtopics. Your job is to identify the subtopics that allow you to incorporate interesting content options. A focused topic will make your content more powerful. In this era of Internet content overload, you have the opportunity to connect with your audience on the topic of most interest to them. The key is to narrow the topic focus in a way that is relevant to your business or project while still holding your audience's interest.

While I do want you to narrow your focus, know that your focus will shift over time. You'll have an opportunity to adjust your focus in each content planning cycle. Don't worry about making any further changes now. You'll have a chance to adapt as your focus shifts over time with trending news, new product lines, or seasonal influences.

Remember you will be most likely to find an audience if you offer content centered on a specific subject. You want to create content that supports the purpose statement created in Step 1. Jot down your topic focus.

1.1 Expertise

As you explore your focus, remember to draw on your expertise. You and your content creators bring specific, relevant experience and knowledge to your content creation team. You can further leverage that expertise through brainstorming and research. We'll talk further about both later in this chapter.

Keep your expertise in mind as you find your focus. What do you know? Creating content allows you to both affirm your authority on a particular topic and establish your authority on related topics. It is essential to draw on your expertise.

1.2 Engagement

Remember also to consider engagement as you hone your focus. Engagement is the process that inspires readers and viewers to interact with content. You want them to click "like," or leave a comment. You also want them to share links to your content with their friends or business associates. They may even quote part of your work in their content.

In turn, your content team has to be responsive. Respond to compliments and criticism. Answer questions. Explore different points of view. Infuse your work with personality, humor, and integrity. Do all of this with good writing, quality audio, and superior images, and your content is likely to have tons of engagement. Remember to be consistent in your engagement with your readers. You can't chat with readers in February and then ignore them until June!

Keep engagement in mind as you set your focus. If you generate content that inspires a response, dialogue or, potentially, action, your message will travel much further. A few adjustments to your focus may increase engagement. For example, a motorcycle retailer may focus solely on the brands of motorcycles it sells. However, I would encourage them to broaden that focus to the motorcycle riders doing charitable work in the community, regardless of what brand they ride.

2. Brainstorming and Research

Now, we turn our attention to the two main methods for finding content ideas: brainstorming and research. I'm going to share a number of techniques to help you brainstorm and research ideas. The goal is to identify and capture lots of potential content ideas for your blog, podcast, or email newsletter. Not every idea will be published but the more ideas you have to choose from, the stronger your content plan will be.

Some of these techniques may be familiar from your artistic, academic, or professional history. Other techniques will be new to you. I encourage you to try a wide range of techniques. Try different things each time you roll through the content planning cycle. See what works for you. Some will inspire and inform your work. It's OK to pick some favorite techniques and stick with them as long as they help you generate new ideas. If you ever find yourself struggling to find new content ideas, revisit this chapter and try a new technique to get you unstuck.

I strongly encourage you to set aside uninterrupted time for brainstorming and research. Gather the people and resources you need to generate ideas. Formalize it on everyone's calendar so you'll have a productive meeting. I suggest you schedule such a session in keeping with your content planning cycle. Adjust the idea generation meeting frequency to parallel your content planning cycle. You many need to meet more or less often depending on the volume of content.

Some offices respect the boundaries of working meetings. If you're lucky enough to work in that environment, work together in a large office space. However, it's OK to get out of the office, if need be. In fact, a new environment may spark new ideas. Try going to a park, a local brew pub, or even a rented boardroom. Moving to a new space can be inspiring and energizing, similar to a vacation.

In addition, be sensitive to the contributions of team members who don't thrive in group meetings. Ensure introverts have the opportunity to add their ideas. Work hard to create an inclusive conversation. To ensure their contributions are heard, allow all contributors, especially shy ones, to share ideas by email or digital workspace before or after the meeting.

Don't limit yourself to the new ideas that pop up in your formal brainstorming and research sessions. Ideas can happen at any time; on your commute, at the theater, in the bathtub. Wherever you are, try to capture the gist of the idea and formalize it at your next opportunity. Encourage your idea team to do the same. To help you capture your brainstorms and research ideas, the workbook in the appendix includes a monthly page to jot down your ideas; or, use your digital workspace solution.

2.1 Overcoming procrastination

Before we move on to brainstorming and research techniques, I want to pause a moment and alert you to the challenges of procrastination. It's the sum of all the little (and big) things you do instead of getting on with your work. You might call your Dad, review your spam folder, or rearrange your office plants. All of these tasks put a barrier between you and the content you're trying to create.

If your procrastination is caused by distractions, do what you can to eliminate them. Speak to the noisy coworker in your open office or move to a quieter work area. If you work from a home office, kids can be a huge distraction during school breaks. Consider shifting your work time to those hours when the kids are sleeping or at activities.

Distractions can also come in tiny packages. You'll know this if you've ever tried typing with a hangnail. Ouch! Find a file, smooth the nail, and eliminate the distraction.

As you expand your efforts to flow through the content planning cycle, it's important to be alert to procrastination. Know that it can block your creative efforts. When you have the urge to check social media feeds, do dust bunny patrol, watch Netflix, or pursue any another distraction, be mindful that you are off course. Being aware of the things you do when you procrastinate will help you get back to work on the project at hand.

2.2 Overcoming writer's block

I also want to alert you to the problem of writer's block. Sometimes content creators struggle to write, record, or photograph. They are paralyzed into inaction. Nothing is getting done. It's a frightening moment when you're in the business of creating content. This common phenomenon is called writer's block. Even seasoned content creators have episodes where the pieces just won't come together. Usually the block will pass in its own time but content creators don't always have time to spare before a deadline.

The cause of your writer's block could come from a wide range of sources. You might be struggling with a health issue or worrying about a family member. You might have been creating for too many days in a row and need a break. You might be creating content on a topic that bores you. The pressure of a looming deadline can overwhelm any skills you have to get things done.

Of course, there are dozens more potential problems that can cause writer's block. Whatever your triggers, one or more of the following techniques will help you overcome the problem.

- Breathe. Take a moment to focus on your breath. Inhale deeply, hold the air a moment, and then exhale slowly.

- Eat and drink. You might be dehydrated or have low blood sugar. Fuel your body.

- Step away. Move from your desk or studio and do something else. Take care of your filing, or make a cup of coffee. Keep your hands busy.

- Take a nap. A 20-minute power snooze can reset your brain. You'll return refreshed. But be sure to set an alarm. Sleep any longer and you'll wake up feeling groggy.

- Switch tools. If you usually write on a computer, get out a pen and notebook and try handwriting for a while.

- Doodle or color. Adult coloring can help you focus. As you color a design, your subconscious mind calms itself and rejuvenates.

You may have noticed the coloring border on each monthly brainstorming page in the workbook in the appendix. For years, I've spent a few minutes doodling or coloring with fine art supplies as a brain break. I invite you to do the same.

- Create a writing ritual. If you do the same things each time you sit down at your desk, your mind may flow into writing mode. Your ritual might include turning on a special desk lamp, tidying the desk surface, and finding your favorite pen.

- Warm up your words. Just as you need to stretch before exercise, a writing warm-up can help you get started. I'm fond of question journals where you jot down a few lines to briefly answer the question of the day.

- Break it down. Split a big task into smaller tasks. Break it into pieces. Do 100 words, or three photographs. Sometimes the whole thing in one go can be daunting.

- Make a checklist. Enjoy the satisfaction of ticking off a box on the list as each content creation task is complete.

- Surf the web. Peruse websites and online magazines that are unrelated to your topic. Give your brain a mini-vacation. If you do hop online, avoid social media. It's hard to break free once you start scrolling through newsfeeds.

- Get some exercise. A walk, a swim, some yoga, or a trip to the gym will rejuvenate your body and jumpstart your mind. Make sure to choose an exercise you enjoy.

- Go to a library or bookstore. Browse the stacks. See what's on the bestseller list. Dig around in the discount bin. Other writers' successes can inspire.

- Have a conversation. Talk to someone about your topic. Introduce your subject to a listener who knows nothing about it, or deepen your own knowledge in conversation with an expert in your field.

- Play with desk toys. The playful treasures hidden in your desk give your hands something to do. As you fidget with a toy your mind calms and your ability to focus on the task at hand improves.

- Change locations. My grandmother often shared the wisdom that "a change is as good as a rest" and I agree. Take your laptop to a coffee shop, a park, or even just a different location within your space.

Your ability to create could also be stalled by your own inner critic, that voice in your head that doubts your abilities. That niggling voice tells you can't write, can't draw, and nobody wants to look at your work so why bother creating it in the first place. It's amazing how quickly that voice can undermine your self confidence and take you off track. As a remedy, I like Ranbir Puar's approach. She said, "You can turn down the volume on your inner critic and turn up your inner champion." Find your inner critic's volume switch and press mute. Listen to your inner champion. You've got this!

3. Brainstorming Techniques

Brainstorming is about seeking out new ideas and capturing their essence in the moment. It's about taking what you already have and exploring new ways to expand. Effective brainstorming should draw out all the ideas no matter how crazy or unusual or mundane. One idea sparks another. One contributor builds off another's idea. An analyst shares an interesting discovery that inspires more content. No idea is too big or too small. No idea is judged or dismissed at this phase. Brainstorming techniques allow you to capture a full range of ideas that can be evaluated and ranked later.

Be alert that this is an area of content planning where you might be tempted to skip ahead. Grownups have often forgotten the fourth grade joy of asking questions. Open-ended wonder questions don't get the attention they deserve when we get swept up in the busyness of a work day. To inspire participation, brainstorming sessions have to be fun, lively, and time-bound. Ask your participants to commit to the process. Who knows what will appear?

> For some people, brainstorming is an energizing process filled with possibilities. Yet others loathe the prospect and shy away from anything to do with generating new ideas. Wherever your feelings fall on this spectrum, I ask you to keep an open mind. Explore the techniques below. Some will work well for you and others won't be as successful. The right mix is as personal as your playlist. The goal is to let the ideas flow without judgment or fear. It's OK to be silly and extravagant. Give your imagination a chance to experience wonder in a safe space. You'll likely be surprised at the results.

3.1 Prepare for your session

As you prepare for your brainstorming session, ensure you have all you need for a successful meeting. This includes:

- Formal agenda
- Rules for brainstorming
- Refreshments
- Computer, whiteboard, flip chart, or notebook
- Office supplies
- Technique supplies

As with any meeting, a formal agenda communicates the start and stop time for the meeting. Be respectful of people's time! It indicates the flow of activities and states when breaks will be taken. Knowing how their time is planned helps participants be present and focused on the brainstorming in progress.

The rules for brainstorming should always request attendees' willingness to participate in the process. Also, ask for mutual understanding that you are creating a respectful environment where everyone can be heard. All ideas are worthy and given equal consideration. Beyond that, the rules for brainstorming need to draw on your organization's work style. For example, you might ask participants to put their mobile devices in airplane mode to reduce distractions. Conversely, you might invite participants to Instagram the process. Here are some example rules:

- Be present.

- All ideas are welcome.

- Everyone's voice is equal.

- Listen to understand, not respond.

- Expand on others' ideas.

- No judgments here.

- Don't block ideas.

- Capture everything.

Plan to develop your rules for brainstorming early in your meeting agenda. Be sure to share them with new team members to help them quickly understand your structure. If your team meets regularly and has established a set of rules like this, review the rules at every idea generation meeting.

Refreshments are always a good idea at meetings. Basic water, coffee, and tea is fine to ensure your team stays hydrated. If your budget allows, add food to keep participants' blood sugar up. Fruit, vegetables, and protein are your best choices. Carbohydrates like pastries or candy can make your team wound-up and then sleepy, which is not ideal for brainstorming! A shared meal can keep the team together during breaks. Often, further ideas come up in this unstructured time.

Next, you'll need a way to capture all your content ideas. Some of the techniques, such as mind maps, record ideas as part of the process. Other techniques may need a formal note-taker using a computer, tablet, or paper notebook. This could be a volunteer from the team or someone who observes the process and acts as recording secretary. Team members can also take turns adding ideas to whiteboards or flip charts in the meeting space.

Make sure you have lots of office supplies on hand. Nothing disrupts a session like the hunt for a working whiteboard marker. If you're not sure what you'll need, start with note pads, sticky notes, tape, pencils, pens, and markers in different colors. As your team finds its brainstorming mojo, you can add anything that's missing during the formal breaks. Once you figure out what office supplies work for you, I suggest creating and keeping a brainstorming toolkit in a file box or desk drawer. That way you won't have to hunt for pens and so on next time.

Last, you may need some technique-specific supplies. This could be anything from word clouds and pipe cleaners to LEGO and game dice. We're going to talk about several techniques in this chapter. As you select techniques for your brainstorming session, make note of any supplies you'll need.

We've set the stage for your brainstorming meeting and the participants are ready to go. But what to do? Give your brainstorming structure with a brainstorming technique. Many techniques are intended for a group working together but they can be adapted for someone brainstorming alone, if you're working on your own.

Brainstorming can be as simple as a conversation amongst colleagues bouncing ideas around. A chat and a notepad or tablet to jot down each idea is the minimum required. Beyond that, more formal brainstorming sessions can tap into one or more techniques to spark ideas and make the process fun. Let's explore a few of my favorites.

3.2 Mind maps

A mind map helps you identify and explore interconnected ideas. Sticky notes on a wall, a large whiteboard, or blank bulletin boards with a supply of push-pins can all be used to capture and visualize ideas. There are also tools like MindMeister (www.mindmeister.com) or Evernote that help you create digital mind maps. For now, let's assume that we're using a large whiteboard.

To create a mind map, you start with a central or core topic. In the context of a content plan, that's your focus topic. That focus topic is placed at the center of your whiteboard surrounded by a circle. From that central idea, new ideas branch out in a ripple effect. Be sure to project the map as you create it for all participants to see. Alternatively, you can go analog with pencil on paper. For example, Sample 3 is a mind map I drew for my vintage toy blog project, Toy Rhapsody.

What ideas spark from your focus topic? What can you create to support your purpose statement? Use the mind map technique to capture your ideas and see how they are interconnected.

Toy Rhapsody is a blog I'm writing for fun. I use it to celebrate play and encourage us all to stretch our imaginations. It's a labor of love based on my own childhood toys growing up in the 1970s and 1980s. I mention it here as I've used it as a case study to illustrate the brainstorming techniques described in this book. If you'd like to read it, visit www.toy-rhapsody.com.

SAMPLE 3: MIND MAP

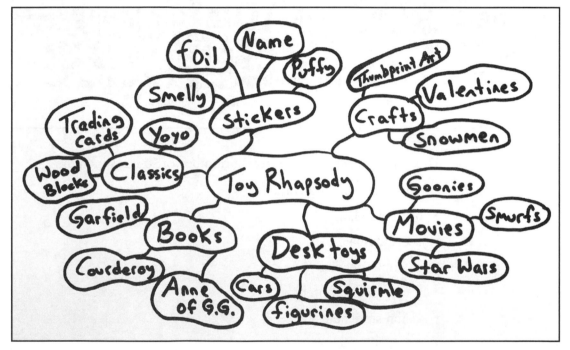

3.3 Thought clouds

Another brainstorming approach is to generate thought clouds. Thought clouds are also known as word clouds. Once generated, your brainstorming team can review the thought cloud to see what words have been featured before. The larger the words the more often they appear in your input texts. Your team can also assess the juxtaposition of various words within the cloud to spark new brainstorms.

I like Jonathan Feinberg's free tool at www.wordle.net to create thought clouds. To use this tool, copy and paste existing documents into the word cloud generator. For example, the word cloud in Sample 4 was generated with the text from six of my Toy Rhapsody blog posts.

SAMPLE 4: THOUGHT CLOUD

The text you use could be from a number of sources including:

- previously created content,
- business plan,
- user manuals,
- customer feedback,
- social media content,
- vision statement, or
- product launch materials.

Choose documents related to your topic. You want the resulting thought cloud to be relevant to the content you hope to create. Once entered, the JavaScript at Wordle generates an image of words. You can manipulate the orientation, language, font, layout, and color of your thought cloud. Use the default or make adjustments until it's visually pleasing.

3.4 Wonder questions

Next, we turn to open-ended questions to assist with brainstorming. Classroom teachers call these "wonder questions." Even as adults, that sense of wonder can be very powerful when generating ideas. It allows participants to pose questions that they are curious about. Answering them can make for focused, in-depth content. A true wonder question must ask why or how or what. It goes beyond a binary answer of yes or no.

Ask brainstorming participants and others in your organization to submit questions for consideration. This allows people who know your organization from multiple perspectives to pose relevant questions. You also get to explore curiosity. Maybe the sales department doesn't really understand how manufacturing works? Your team then reviews the questions and prioritizes which to answer and publish as content.

Here are some wonder questions related to Toy Rhapsody, focused on its central topic of vintage toys from the 1970s and 1980s.

- How did Fisher Price select the first play sets it created?

- What kid-friendly games can be played with a deck of cards?

- Why is it so hard to learn to juggle?

- When Crayola retires a crayon color, is there a secondhand market for that color?

- How did Atari market its first game consoles?

If creating your own questions is a struggle, you can turn to question books. There are thousands to choose from. Visit your local bookstore and browse the shelves or simply put "questions" into the search field of your favorite online retailer. Today, Amazon.com has thousands of question books available. If you'd like to narrow your search, two of my favorites are *To Our Children's Children* by Bob Greene & D.G. Fulford (Doubleday, 1998) and *If ... (Questions for the Game of Life)* by Evelyn McFarlane & James Saywell (Villard, 1995).

Each of these books lists hundreds of open-ended, thought-provoking questions. Your brainstorming team can peruse the books looking for questions relevant to your focus topic. There's so much variety you're sure to find something. Once you have some questions, answer them as a group according to the potential content the answer might create.

3.5 Inspiration decks

Sometimes brainstorming makes more progress with visual stimulation. Inspiration decks are a compact and portable way to explore way to share a wide range of visual ideas. One deck may be ideal for your focus topic, or you may choose to use two or more decks for variety and juxtaposition.

Inspiration decks fall into two categories: secular and spiritual. The secular decks are often tied to relationships, happiness, gratitude, creativity, or dozens of other topics. There are hundreds of options listed with online retailers and book stores will often stock options in their self-help or spirituality sections. My favorites include:

- Stormdeck by Tim Porter

- Writer Emergency Pack by John August

- Creative Whack Pack by Roger von Oech

As I mentioned, spiritual inspiration decks are also available. If it's appropriate to your brand or topic, you may want to incorporate one or more spiritual decks into your brainstorming activities. Search for terms like:

- angel cards

- medicine wheel cards

- Tarot cards

- Rune cards

- Celtic cards

Please be aware of the potential for cultural appropriation. You're welcome to draw inspiration from any spiritual practice but use caution in the content you create. Your content plan could harm your brand if you inadvertently use something for commercial purposes out of cultural context.

As an example, I spent 20 minutes perusing a deck of angel cards while brainstorming ideas for Toy Rhapsody. As a result, I added the following brainstorms as potential additions to my content plan:

- A blog post about homemade angel costumes

- A step-by-step photo post about making a paper craft angel

- A post of public domain Christmas carol lyrics

- A post about the historic hanky dolls made during the Civil War

As you can see, the ideas are not specifically about the angels on the cards nor their guiding messages. Rather, this list captures ideas inspired by the things I saw on the angel cards. No matter what deck you use, the goal is to spark ideas for your content plan. Remember to take inspiration from the meaning of the cards and the writing as well as the artwork.

3.6 Touch and move

When brainstorming, it's important to use all your senses, if you can. Don't limit yourself to visual input. Kinesthetic and tactile information can be just as inspiring. Kinesthetic information comes from movement; tactile information from our sense of touch. In either case, we put our bodies in motion to inspire brainstorms.

Sitting at a desk all day may not inspire brainstorming. Get out for a walk in the forest, practice yoga, or hold an impromptu dance party. Try a theater improvisation game, or martial art. Get moving!

Tactile information can come from anything you touch, especially with your hands. Technically, that can include projects like making a backyard hockey rink or shopping for groceries. I recommend you avoid any tactile inputs on a big scale and also avoid familiar tasks. More practically, give your brainstorming team things to explore with their hands. Items that bend and fold and stick together in a variety of ways are ideal. This might include pipe cleaners, clay, building blocks, game dice, or coloring pages. Anything you'd find in an elementary school art class will be cost-effective and enhance brainstorming. Tap into your sense of play.

I spent a happy morning playing with some art supplies to explore brainstorms for Toy Rhapsody. Paper, stickers, and markers indirectly inspired the following ideas:

- Explore why movie studios are remaking so many classic children's films.
- Visit the Vermont Teddy Bear Hospital.
- Find out how jelly beans are made.
- Blog series on the restoration of a 1978 Fisher Price dollhouse.

Kinesthetic and tactile brainstorming tools can inspire ideas directly and indirectly. Your team member may be inspired by his or her experience or what is created. These tools can also keep participants' hands busy as great ideas come to mind in a concurrent discussion.

3.7 Play

I love what Sabrina Furminger expressed at a recent Leading Moms conference. She said, "When you make time for silly it can flush out your mind and inspire your writing." And she's right. Even as adults we need to play sometimes and explore the world the way we did as children. If you're feeling unsure about play at the office, explore this technique at home with your own children. Although I promise you, I've been in offices where an epic NERF war was embraced by the entire team!

With Toy Rhapsody in mind, I spent some time with my son. I didn't tell him about the brainstorming activity. I simply made mental notes of ideas that came as we built a fort, inspected our LEGO mini-figure army, donned dress-up costumes, and raced around the house with toy cars. Here are some ideas that came to mind:

- What are the differences in a toy production standards between 1977 and 2017?

- How are brands like Teenage Mutant Ninja Turtles refreshed for new generations?

- Should vintage toys be kept from children or should they be played with?

- How would my digital-generation child react to the video games I played in 1980?

Play is a great way to find new ideas, even if your topic is not toy related! You'll see universal themes of conflicting personalities: nation building and peacemaking among others. As you play, be alert to themes that emerge and how they might apply to your business.

3.8 Music

Listening to music can inspire in many ways. Music can evoke emotion, recall old memories, and suggest style. In addition, lyrics often tell a universal story and certain phrases are part of our everyday conversation. Auditory input is another way to stimulate your brainstorming team.

One way to use music is to have everyone contribute to a playlist. Alternatively, you can assign one person to prepare a playlist. The list might be music that resonates with team members or it may evoke the topic itself. I've been compiling a list of toy related songs for Toy Rhapsody.

- The Teddy Bears' Picnic

- Let's Go Fly a Kite

- Rubber Duckie

You can use the playlist as background music for your overall brainstorming session or have a music break from time to time. Allow team members to add to your notes as inspiration strikes.

3.9 Plan an outing

Think about the last time your team got out of the office. If you work mostly in the four walls of your office space, get out with your team for a shared experience. Here are some suggested outings that can help you find fresh ideas:

- Visit a museum, art gallery, or science center.

- Go to the movies and see a blockbuster or art film.

- Explore nature at a local park or hiking trail.

- Tour the factory where your products are made.

- Visit an artisan food business and sample their wares.

Capture new ideas during your outing or have a follow-up session to talk over any inspiration. Don't delay! Ideas will fade after the end of the outing.

3.10 Use a facilitator

A brainstorming facilitator can guide your team through one or more brainstorming exercises and take care of the logistics for each session. This frees everyone on your team to participate equally in the most important part of each session: idea generation!

Professional facilitators have training in group dynamics, communication styles, and techniques like the ones I've described here. Depending on your topic focus, a layperson may also be able to serve you well. If you think it will help your team, bring in a brainstorming facilitator to guide your group.

4. Research Techniques

Research is another method to help you find your ideas. Often research follows brainstorming, as you have to find the answer to the questions you've posed or confirm the facts you believe to be true. You can also start with research and create content based on what you find. Let's talk about some research techniques.

4.1 Internet research

When you want to know something these days, I suspect your first stop is Google. Plug in a question or some keywords and thousands of search results come back to you in less than a second. You'll likely find the answer you're looking for on the first page of results. However, it's essential you confirm the website as a reliable source of information.

As you use a search engine, you can refine the results you see by using Boolean search modifiers. These include quotes, parentheses, AND, OR, and NOT.

Depending on the Internet research you undertake, you may be searching in a specialized database such as magazine archive, ancestry documents, or an academic database. Boolean search modifiers work in many situations but be sure to consult the help files of less familiar databases for customized instructions. This will save you frustration.

Use the modifier "AND" (all capital letters) to search for two or more words or phrases together. By default, search engines assume you're looking for all the words you type in the search bar. For example, a search for storm preparedness will bring back similar results as storm AND preparedness.

Use the modifier "OR" (all capital letters) to search for one of two or more words or phrases together. This can help you search for similar terms such as "lawyer OR solicitor."

Use the modifier "NOT" (all capital letters) to search for one or more words or phrases without the word or phrase after the NOT. For example, you could search for "candy NOT mints" to see results for all kinds of candy without any mention of mints.

You also use quotes to search for a particular phrase. Place the quotes around the words that should appear together in the search results. This is especially useful for proper names. For example, search for "sailing hats" and see how the results differ from sailing hats without the quotation marks.

Finally, you can make use of parentheses to search for words that should appear together. For example, search for "(Tilley 'sailing hats') retailers" to find a place to buy your next Tilley hat.

Whatever your topic, Internet search can be great source of research. Remember to look for reliable sources and to employ Boolean modifiers to help improve your search results.

4.2 Content review

Content review is a research method where you look at the content that's already been generated on a given topic. Much of the content may be things your organization has created both for publication and for internal use only. In a content review, you'll also look at the content made public by others creating content on the same topic.

For example, you might publish recipes on your vegetarian food blog. You'll have an archive of all the recipes you've developed — both the ones you've published on your blog and the drafts you're holding back for now. Your content review would look at both your published and draft content. In addition, you would review other food bloggers' sites, food magazines, cookbooks, and food manufacturers' materials.

Review of the content may show gaps in the information available; areas that are underserved; or areas that are too frequently written about. Through your research you can refine your content plan to ensure you are creating new, useful, and relevant content.

4.3 Interviews

Interviews are a most powerful research tools available to content creators and an opportunity to question both experts and consumers.

Interview subject matter experts: people who know your topic. Potential interviewees can include customers, designers, manufacturers, suppliers, retailers, researchers, and anyone else. You can interview more than one person in each category.

For example, you could ask your current customers what challenges they are facing and how they use the information you provide. You can also give them the opportunity to share their wisdom. You never know how their hopes, dreams, and ideas can flow into your content plan. In fact, your research interview could become a biography piece in your content plan. Think of it as a "getting to know you" feature.

Whoever you're interviewing, make good use of your time with them. Most of all be respectful of their time! If you ask for a 30-minute interview, don't take a minute extra. In fact, I'd encourage you to finish your interview 5 minutes early, if you can.

If possible, research the interviewee a little bit in advance. You may find something on a website or social network that reveals common interests. You can use that information to establish rapport which will make the interview process a more natural conversation.

Be sure to prepare some questions in advance, as well. Use those questions as a framework for the conversation but don't hesitate to ask additional follow-up questions based on the answers you hear.

4.4 Surveys

I highly recommend surveys as a useful research tool. Use surveys to capture information about your topic, your audience, and the industry or community you serve. A carefully crafted survey can provide fodder for many different content pieces.

Different tools allow you to create online surveys. Free options include Google Forms and Survey Monkey. Paid tools like Infusionsoft and Tradable Bits also include survey functionality. In some cases, the tools (both free and paid) can integrate into your customer relationship management (CRM) system or social tracking dashboard. Pick the tool that integrates best with the tools you're already using as an organization.

As you create your survey, include some short answer or multiple choice questions so that respondents can progress through the survey quickly. Also include one or two open-ended questions where respondents can write longer, more thoughtful responses. Try to keep your survey succinct and ask only the essential questions. There's no firm rule on how many questions you ask but I try to keep it at fewer than a dozen questions for any survey I create.

To encourage honest participation, I suggest you give respondents the opportunity to reply anonymously. If you do ask for a name or email address, respect that information: Only add the contact to your database if you've explicitly requested and received their permission in the survey.

Depending on the group you want to take the survey, you may have to incentivize them with a thank-you gift or chance to enter a draw for a prize. If appropriate, you can offer to share a copy of the results as a token of appreciation. Other groups will participate without the perk.

Keep the survey open for a set period of time. While the survey is live, promote it through email, social media, and word of mouth to encourage responses. Once the survey time period has expired, close it.

The analysis of the information is the next phase for survey research. Your survey tool may provide some preliminary analysis and often graphs or charts representing the replies. Someone on your content creation team should also review the numbers and read all the open-ended responses. Look for information that can be added to your content plan.

Turn survey information into a video series answering common questions, or publish photographs explaining how to use a product. You can also make content by creating one or more infographics.

4.5 Numbers analysis

Numbers analysis is your opportunity to think like a stockbroker. You'll look for trends and the unexpected in figures related to your topic. Numbers tell a story and it's a specialized skill to be able to read that story.

You'll need to gather numbers related to your topic. Sales figures, viewership, manufacturing volumes, anything you can count can be included. Look for the same information for each year over a period of time. This will allow you to explore how the numbers change over time.

Then review the numbers and look for trends. What areas show growth? Where have you taken losses? Is there a reason for a surge? The information you uncover can become a source of content ideas.

4.6 Archives

If your topic lends itself to historical research, dive into the archives. You may have a corporate archive or access to a relevant city archive. Archival research requires care and attention. Your quest for inspiration must be respectful of the past.

Research techniques can be created to approach any topic and help identify ideas for your content plan. Often content creators will return to research at regular intervals to update the information collected.

5. Use the Ideas from Your Brainstorming and Research

Once you've identified a full range of ideas, they can be combined and morphed into new and interesting content. The ideas that are in keeping with your purpose, speak from your authority, and engage your audience should be assigned to your editorial calendar. We'll talk about how to do that in Step 5.

6

Step 5:
Make an Editorial Calendar

With your collection of ideas generated in Step 4, it's time to schedule content on your editorial calendar. With the information in this chapter, you'll be able to organize and prioritize your ideas. You'll also schedule your publication dates and include time for pre-publication tasks and post-publication activities. An editorial calendar is about much more than the day your content becomes visible to your audience.

1. Your Editorial Calendar

An editorial calendar is a dated document that notes when you will prepare each piece of content, when it will be published, and the post-publication tasks necessary to complete the content planning cycle. Your calendar can be paper or electronic. Some people start with a paper calendar, then transcribe that information to digital format for easy sharing. Others type everything directly into an electronic calendar.

Use whatever method suits your work style. It's a personal choice and it is okay to experiment to find the method that works best for you.

Any calendar is great for content planning as long as you use one! *The Content Planner* includes a fill-in-the-blank editorial calendar in the appendix (and on the download kit) with month-at-a-glance sheets. Start with that to help you execute your content plan, if you like.

Some people disagree with the wisdom of writing out an editorial calendar. As an alternative, they prefer to use task lists and assignments to get the needed work done. That's a legitimate work flow. However, I think there's power in writing things down if you want to be consistent in your content success. I also prefer the visual to see an overview of all content pieces. This is why I recommend you formalize your plans in a calendar.

When it comes to calendars, you have many options. Your computer, mobile phone, and tablet all have calendar options. Many of those are backed up and synced across devices through systems like Google Calendar, iCloud, or other online services. Add to that the plethora of printed options available at any office supply store: date books, desk calendars, wall calendars, and other formats are available for purchase in a variety of colors, sizes, and styles.

An electronic calendar in any format makes it easier to share the information with a group so all your content contributors can see the master plan. This helps individuals schedule time in their personal calendars to keep track of their contributions to the content plan. The bigger your content team, the more complicated it can be to keep track of what's happening. Even a small team or individual creating lots of content needs to keep track of what's happening.

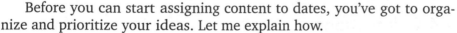

In Step 2: Know Your Audience, we discussed the different content collaborators who might be part of your team. Make sure you've included all the necessary collaborators in the process.

Before you can start assigning content to dates, you've got to organize and prioritize your ideas. Let me explain how.

2. Organize Your Ideas

Throughout your brainstorming and research sessions, you captured many ideas for your content plan. Now is the time to review those ideas and explore how you might present the content. To begin, you need context for your content. The specifics of content creation as text, images, audio, or video will follow in Step 6.

In this step, you want to think in broad terms. Consider each topic and contemplate if it's best as evergreen content, a one-hit wonder, or something else. In this section, I'll show you some of the most useful presentation contexts.

2.1 Evergreen content

Content that is evergreen never gets stale or out of date. It's always relevant and useful. Informative evergreen content often becomes one of the most viewed posts on a website or blog. It contains content that the audience wants to reference regularly. Examples include a food safety website with instructions for cooking a turkey; an artist's blog with tips to prepare pages with gesso; or a landscaping page with tips on how to winterize your shrubs.

2.2 One-hit wonders

By contrast, some great ideas don't really fit anywhere else. Like a one-time chart-topping song, you will occasionally say yes to your one-hit wonder. It may be clever, quirky, funny, or otherwise unique. It may tell your story in a different way. Whatever it is, there's room for this idea in your content plan. Examples include a video of a famous musician jamming with buskers in a subway station; an improvised sock puppet play; or a kayaker's dolphin pod encounter.

2.3 Biographies

If your brainstorms and research include people-related information, biographical posts can be a boon to your content plan. For example, a car manufacturer may post about its founder; a scientific laboratory might introduce its inventor; or a child safety organization might profile a volunteer advocate. Whoever you profile helps personalize your brand.

For some organizations, the content plan includes a lot of content about the people involved. This can include both staff and volunteers as well as people served by the organization or those who use the product.

2.4 Celebrations

Think beyond the traditional seasonal and religious celebrations. Instead, look at your brainstorms and research milestones. For example, celebrate 25 years of service to your organization, the resilience needed to still be in business after the challenges of a flood ruined your inventory, or the launch of new service offering with the story of its creation.

2.5 Be of service

With your persona in mind, content can be of service to your audience. Help your reader solve a problem. For example, a gardener's tutorial on preventing damage to your lawn, a primer on make-up techniques for high-definition video, or a baker's tips on baking a fruitcake.

2.6 Events

As a category of content, events include both those your organization hosts as well as events you are attending such as trade shows and conferences. These might include product launch parties, family celebrations, plus speaking and sponsorship opportunities. Events create opportunities for content before, during, and after the event. Event-related content is an extension of your relationship and networking efforts.

2.7 Product features

If your topic is centered on a product or service, some content must be created to highlight functions and benefits. In this category, provide advance information about upcoming projects, factory tours, and demonstrations. Often a business has multiple products in various stages of development. Use this context to include content about each of them on your editorial calendar.

2.8 Regulatory

On occasion, content fulfills regulatory requirements. You may be required to post your terms of service, safety notices, or product warnings. Use this category to ensure you are making reasonable efforts to communicate regulatory information to your audience.

2.9 Make your own

Finally, I want to remind you that the categories I've listed to provide context to organize your ideas are only the beginning. You'll see other groupings in your content ideas and, over time, patterns will emerge.

3. Prioritize Your Content

After considering ways you can organize your content, you've probably got more ideas than you can use right away. That's great! Lots of options give you the opportunity to include variety in the content you publish. As you prioritize your content, use your editorial calendar to plug content into tentative publication dates. This will give you a visual to assess the pace at which each piece of content will be published.

3.1 Time sensitive

First, schedule time-sensitive content that supports a time-bound business or project activity. This might include a product launch, a change of personnel, a new version release, a fashion season, a public appearance, or some other time-sensitive content.

3.2 Seasonal

Next, schedule anything that's seasonal. For example, festive New Year greetings or back to school themes only make sense at certain times. If you're a food blogger, pumpkin recipes make more sense in the fall than they do in early spring.

3.3 Series

Next, consider your commitment to any ongoing series. If you do regular book reviews or interviews with industry experts, then be sure to publish more content in the series. If you usually publish one piece of content a month that supports your series then be sure you've scheduled something relevant on your editorial calendar. Series may publish daily, weekly, monthly, quarterly, or annually, at your discretion.

3.4 Frequency

Finally, look at your overall frequency. You may need to postpone some content because you've scheduled more than you can create and support in the time available. Look for gaps in your editorial calendar, too. You may need to add some more content. Adjust as needed to support your purpose statement and serve your audience.

There's disagreement amongst content marketing experts about the ideal frequency of publishing. Some say you have to publish three times a week without fail. Others say publish only when you've got inspired, meaningful content to share. There really is no single frequency that's perfect for every situation. Depending on the project, my advice usually falls somewhere in the middle of that spectrum. Experiment with frequency until you find that sweet spot that works for your audience and your business. Think of frequency as a spectrum from once a quarter, to monthly, to weekly, to daily, and variations in between.

Also, remember that your frequency may vary depending on your platform. If you publish to a primary and then supplemental platforms, the frequency for your website or blog will almost certainly be different than what's needed for your email newsletter or podcast.

As you contemplate how often to publish content, keep in mind your audience. You want to provide them with timely information but they may unsubscribe if the content you share comes too frequently or they may forget who you are if content comes too rarely. Find that ideal frequency for your audience. Your audience is made up of many different types of content consumers. You'll have to pick the frequency that serves the majority, but you won't be able to please everyone.

Your purpose should also impact your frequency. A graphic designer who sets his or her purpose to build an online portfolio could safely publish new content once a month. In contrast, a candy shop will want to publish at least once a week to support its core purpose of candy sales.

You also need to make the frequency decision knowing your content creation resources. How much time do you have for writing, recording, editing, formatting, publishing, and promotion? The more often you publish the more resources you need to execute all of those tasks. Can you afford that much time in human resources?

Take good care of your brand. Publishing poor content too often can hurt it and contradict the brand building you're doing by publishing content. Ideally, you'll publish great content with the right frequency to support and build your brand.

3.5 Opportunity knocks

Before you lock down your editorial calendar, leave room in your content plan to add to the conversation about current events, celebrity news, weather anomalies, or serendipitous meetings. You never know when circumstance will put you in the position to create a wonderful but unexpected piece of content.

Spontaneous content is usually not scheduled in advance on the content plan. This content can be both joyous and somber. Joyous events like a new baby, a prestigious award, or a notable mention in mainstream media should be shared. Somber events such as a terror attack, a natural disaster, or death of a world figure might also work. When it fits with your purpose and is of interest to your audience, it's appropriate to leave room in your editorial calendar for spontaneous content.

4. Make Your Schedule

An editorial calendar is more than just a list of publication dates. Each piece of content needs a schedule to support it. The schedule outlines the work to be done before and after the publication date. Pre-publication, you must take time to create the content and prepare it to be shared with

SAMPLE 5: CALENDAR WORKSHEET

January

Sunday	Monday	Tuesday	Wednesday	Thursday	Friday	Saturday
1	2 Blog #1	3	4 Blog #2	5	6	7
8	9	10 Email #1	11	12	13 Podcast #1	14
15	16 Blog #3	17	18 Blog #4	19	20	21
22	23	24 Email #2	25	26	27 Podcast #2	28
29	30 Blog #5	31				

Notes:

your audience. Post-publication you need time to share your content, engage with your audience, and conduct analysis to inform your next content planning cycle. The schedule is specific about when each content-related task will be done.

Your schedule gives you a framework to organize each content creation team member's contributions. It specifies deadlines. Often the next step of content creation is contingent on the previous step being complete. Tasks will overlap, especially if you have multiple pieces of content to publish in a given month (or whatever duration your content planning cycle runs). When you work on more than one piece of content at the same time, each will be a different phase in the schedule.

Use the calendar pages in the appendix or from the download kit, or your own calendar solution, to map out your content plan.

4.1 Estimate Effort

Before you start adding tasks to your editorial calendar, it's helpful to become familiar with the time and effort needed to complete each task. Project managers often use Gantt charts to understand the work ahead. A Gantt chart is a visual representation of the tasks and how they are scheduled in relation to one another.

You won't need to produce a Gantt chart or similar with every content planning cycle. I encourage you to create one on your first cycle so have a sense of the amount of time needed. On future cycles, you can update those estimates any time you make major changes. Often this is necessary when you change to a different type of content or adjust the frequency of publishing.

Start with an estimate of how many hours you need for brainstorming and research. Then consider the hours needed to create your content and prepare it for publication. Think also about how much time you'll spend on promotion, engagement, and analysis after it's published. As you estimate, think only of the total time required, not the dates when the work will be done. This will help you schedule all the pieces.

Table 1 an example of the effort required for a blog post. Please note that the brainstorming and research estimate reflects a portion of a longer session where many ideas were generated.

Based on your estimates, you'll know how long it will take you to do each phase of content creation and the total time needed. In the example shown, we need a total of 480 minutes, or 8 hours. With the total effort in mind, you can schedule time on your Gantt chart or directly on

TABLE 1: EFFORT ESTIMATE

Effort Estimate

Task	Minutes
Brainstorming/research	15
First draft	60
Edits	30
Take photo	30
Add photo	15
Publication	30
Approval	15
Upload	15
Format	15
Tagging	15
Testing	15
Sharing	45
Promotion	60
Engagement	60
Analysis	60
Total	**480**

your editorial calendar. Let's say you've got four hours a week to work on creating the blog post in our example. And you have eight hours of work to prepare a piece of content for publication and complete its promotion. In this case, the pre-publication tasks should be spread over two weeks in advance of your publication date. And you may want to schedule the work over three weeks so that you have extra time as a contingency. Your effort estimates allow you to plan the correct amount of lead time in advance of publishing a piece of content.

The effort estimates can be represented on a Gantt chart or on your editorial calendar. As I mentioned, the first time through the content planning cycle it can be helpful to prepare a Gantt chart so ensure you have a strong grasp of the task scheduling involved. If you've got some content scheduling experience, you'll be able to plan time directly on your editorial calendar. As always, use that work flow that works best for your content creation team.

The processes I describe in this book are based on traditional project management techniques. They are proven successful and work for many content creation teams. However, there are other approaches to content plan scheduling. If you're looking for alternatives for your team, I suggest you explore agile and scrum project management where the focus shifts from the project to the people. Work is completed in sprints followed by short breaks. Another alternative is Kanban where all tasks are listed on a project board in categories such as open, planned, in progress, testing, and complete. There is always, relentlessly something for every Kanban team member to do.

To populate your schedule, start with the publication date. Next, add the pre-publication activities including brainstorming and research, content creation, formatting, and uploading. Then, schedule the post-publication activities including sharing, promotion, engagement, and analysis.

See how the time for the tasks on our sample blog post would look on a Gantt chart in Sample 6.

SAMPLE 6: GANTT CHART

															May															
Week 1						Week 2							Week 3							Week 4							Week 5			
1	2	3	4	5	6	7	8	9	10	11	12	13	14	15	16	17	18	19	20	21	22	23	24	25	26	27	28	29	30	31
M	T	W	R	F	S	S	M	T	W	R	F	S	S	M	T	W	R	F	S	S	M	T	W	R	F	S	S	M	T	W

Generate ideas
Create content
Approval
Publication date
Sharing & promotion
Engagement
Analysis

And here's how the same tasks for our sample blog post would be documented on an editorial calendar, in Sample 7.

SAMPLE 7: CALENDAR WORKSHEET

May

Sunday	Monday	Tuesday	Wednesday	Thursday	Friday	Saturday
	1	2	3	4	5	6
		generate ideas				
7	8	9	10	11	12	13
		create content				
14	15	16	17	18	19	20
	approval			Blog Published		
21	22	23	24	25	26	27
	sharing & promotion			engagement		
28	29	30	31			
		Analysis				

Notes:

Some content creators do this in project management software such as Basecamp, Trello, or any one of dozens of other similar apps. Search for "project management software" if you're shopping for a digital tool.

One more thing: A big reason to develop a content plan is to focus your content creation efforts. It's important to understand the scope of the work to be completed. It's equally important to decline or defer content creation that's outside of your plan. Understanding the effort involved in creating each piece of content will help you know when to say no. Once you know how much time you need to create your content, you can then move on to scheduling that time for specific dates.

4.2 Pick publication dates

If you haven't already, pick your content topics for this planning cycle and select a publication date for each piece. Choosing your publication dates should follow the priority sequence outlined in section 3. Use the editorial calendar in the appendix, a Gantt chart, or your own scheduling tool to slot your content into specific publication dates.

You might need one piece of content for each blog post you publish. If you publish twice a week on Monday and Thursday, you need two content ideas per week. Alternatively, if you are creating content for an email newsletter, you might need 5 pieces of content for each issue. Publish your newsletter once a month and you'll need 5 content ideas. Publish once a week and you'll 20 ideas each month. You need to select your dates so that you can schedule time for the pre-publication and post-publication tasks.

4.3 Schedule time to create

We're going to talk in detail about creating content when we get to Step 6. Common content creation tasks include writing copy, recording audio files or video, and gathering images. You'll spend time editing your work, proofreading the details, and preparing your content for publication with tags, keywords, and so on. You'll also need lead time in advance of your publication date for any review or approval processes you have in place. This is just an overview of common content creation tasks that may need to be scheduled. Include time for these tasks on your editorial calendar in advance of your publication date.

> Build in extra time for potential delays. You never know when a colleague will fall ill or a technology failure will impact your work. If you work well in advance, you'll still be able to publish on time.

4.4 Schedule time to share and interact

Once you've published your content, you need time to share your content with your audience. We'll talk in detail about this in Step 7. Your efforts will include time to share the content with your true fans plus social media efforts to reach out to your audience. You may also schedule in-person events in support of your content. In the days, or even weeks, after your content is published, you'll need to schedule time to interact with your audience and engage them in conversation. Include time for these tasks on your editorial calendar after your publication date.

4.5 Schedule time to update plans

Finally, you'll want to schedule analysis time. You can assess each individual piece of content or look at the results from an entire content cycle as a whole. Gather the data that's relevant to your purpose. This might include growth in your audience, the amount of engagement, or technical issues. Whatever you learn should inform your next content planning cycle.

Many content creators like to work in advance. There's less stress if a few content pieces are already scheduled. No need to feel the pressure of deadlines. It's also possible to work further ahead so that you can schedule content to go out while one or more members of your content creation team are on vacation.

7

Step 6:
Create Your Content

With an editorial calendar in place, you now know when you need to publish your content. But in order to publish on schedule you've got to create that content. You may do it during office hours, or work when inspiration strikes, even if that's at 3:00 a.m. Everyone has a different productive time. Make the most of yours as you create your content.

1. What Media for the Message?

With your topic in mind, it's time to decide what medium to use. Consider whether your idea is best expressed in text, photographs, graphics, audio, or video. Think also about your platform and what media can be used most effectively. Don't forget your audience, too. You've got to create content in a format that suits their needs.

It's likely you'll create the same piece of content in several ways. Your primary and secondary platforms will need different formats. It's efficient to create all the content at the same time.

A gardener might create content about planting fall bulbs, maybe starting with a text piece about types of bulbs, where to buy, when and how to plant, and so on. The text could be supplemented with photographs of planting. During the photo shoot, he could capture a video tutorial of the same healthy bulb planting. As he creates the content, the gardener could also create an infographic about suggested bulb plantings showing groupings of tulips and daffodils. As you can see, the gardener has the choice to create the content in on one or more media. He can also make the choice to limit the media used. Text and photographs only may be ideal for his platform and audience. The choice is up to the content creator.

Limiting your content creation efforts is often a practical decision. Our gardener can save the expense of extra collaborators to shoot the video and make the infographic. It's okay to choose just one medium if that's what works best for you and your audience.

Whatever media you choose, you'll find advice for making the best content possible in this chapter, as well as some legal considerations.

2. Quality

When creating content, you should create the best quality possible given the skills, time, and other resources available to you and your team.

The quality of the work you create and publish should reflect your brand. This includes adhering to standards for grammar, colors, logo use, sound quality, and so on. As you create content, various quality control procedures will be part of your activity. Quality control may also include an approval process. If you work alone, your quality control check is a conversation with yourself. Large organizations often require the approval of a manager or executive before a piece of content is published. Typically, this individual has not been involved with the content creation process and can offer a fresh perspective.

On occasion, you may stumble across a valuable opportunity to create content. (See Chapter 6, section 3.5, Opportunity Knocks.) You may meet a community leader at the farmers' market while you buy produce. You don't have all your tools on hand but you still want to capture the moment. That's OK. If you see value in the content for your audience, make every attempt to capture the content in the best quality possible.

If the community leader is willing, use your smartphone or whatever other tools you have on hand to record content. Take advantage of the moment. Do a quick interview. Take photos. Record a video. The content may not have the perfect lighting, sound, or video quality but it's still worth sharing. I encourage you to set standards with some flexibility to allow you to take advantage of opportunities as they arise.

Even the content you create with your best tools and the skills of your collaborators might not be the quality you hope to achieve. You may decide to publish content that's the best quality you can manage even if it's not the standard of quality you want to achieve. This is common for businesses with limited resources, and for established businesses experimenting with new ideas. I encourage you to publish some reasonable quality content rather than waiting until you can achieve perfection.

There's a learning process in creating content. Over time, you'll figure out camera angles and text styles that work for you. Capture the best quality content you can, and publish it!

3. Writing Copy

The text components of your content need to start by expressing the idea you want to convey. As Bosco Anthony advises, "Copywriting needs to be real, concise and include a call to action." You may write several paragraphs, short photo captions, or something in between. Write the first draft freely. Focus on what you want to say and add polish later.

Start with good grammar. If you've forgotten the nuances of subject-verb agreement, misplaced modifiers, and other grammatical lessons, take a continuing education course or get a book on the topic.

Correct spelling will add further shine to your text. Brace yourself for controversy when it comes to spelling. For American English, I recommend *The Merriam-Webster Dictionary* as your standard. For British English, I suggest the *Oxford English Dictionary* and, when writing for a Canadian audience, turn to the *Oxford Canadian Dictionary*.

You'll also want to make your text web-friendly. Writing for the Internet is both art and science, but it's still just words on the page. Keep sentences short, use simple sentence structures, write familiar words. Be specific in your language by using concrete nouns and active verbs, and be cautious with pronouns to ensure meaning is clear. Aim for simplicity.

As you write, keep your audience in mind. If needed, refer back to the persona you created. Look at the level of education and the conditions under which the audience will consume your content. Write for a global audience. Make your work accessible. Include slang only if you're certain your audience will understand the reference. Most often it's best to rewrite the content to avoid the slang expression. Don't assume that your audience speaks English as their first language.

In some cases content might be translated into one or more languages. If you start with high-quality text in your primary language and hire a professional translator, a quality translation can result. Translators are in demand and the best ones can be expensive to hire. Don't rely on translation software if you want a polished result.

3.1 Keywords

Ensure your text includes keywords or keyword phrases, as appropriate to your content. The proper use of keywords is an essential task in Search Engine Optimization (SEO). SEO helps your audience find your content. It also helps establish you as an authority on selected keywords.

Each piece of content should include appropriate keywords. Often the keyword expands to a short keyword phrase. The keywords are the part of your content you want to rank for in search engines. When your audience puts that keyword into a search engine your content appears in the search results. Ideally it appears on the first page of search results but building a reputation for popular keywords can take time.

Google AdWords offers a free tool to research keywords and keyword phrases. To use the Keyword Planner tool you will need a free Google account. You can use the same account you use for Gmail, Google Drive, Google Calendar, or any other Google product, including YouTube.

Based on your content topic, you'll enter a keyword or keyword phrase. Use your instinct. Enter your best guess and see what comes up. The results page will show you how your keyword phrase performs in terms of the average monthly searches, the level of competition, and the suggested bid to advertise to those keywords. It also lists related keywords and keyword phrases for your consideration.

See the results when I enter the keyword phrase "vintage toys" in Sample 8.

Based on this information, I can see between 1,000 and 10,000 people search for this phrase each month and that the competition for this keyword phrase is high. It also shows me alternate phrases such as antique toys, retro toys, and collectible toys.

Based on your keyword research, you should change your text to take advantage of a keyword phrase.

SEO-enabled content management tools guide you through the keyword process. (I use the Yoast SEO plugin for WordPress.) Typically,

SAMPLE 8: KEYWORD PLANNER

Google AdWords	Home	Campaigns	Opportunities	Reports	Tools

Keyword Planner
Add ideas to your plan

Your product or service

vintage toys	Get ideas	Modify search

Targeting [?]

All locations	✎
English	✎
Google	✎
Negative keywords	✎

Date range [?]

Show avg. monthly searches for: last 12 months	✎

Customize your search [?]

Keyword filters	✎
Keyword options Show broadly related ideas Hide keywords in my account Hide keywords in my plan	✎
Keywords to include	✎

Average monthly searches for all ideas.
1M – 10M

Ad group ideas	Keyword ideas			Columns ▾	⬇ Download	Add all (490)

Search terms	Avg. monthly searches [?]	Competition [?]	Suggested bid [?]	Ad impr.	Add to plan
vintage toys	1K – 10K	High	CA$0.41		»

Show rows: 30 ▾   1 – 1 of 1 keywords |< < > >|

Keyword (by relevance)	Avg. monthly searches [?]	Competition [?]	Suggested bid [?]	Ad impr.	Add to plan
antique toys	1K – 10K	High	CA$0.41		»
retro toys	1K – 10K	High	CA$0.29		»
vintage toys for sale	100 – 1K	High	CA$0.86		»
collectible toys	1K – 10K	High	CA$0.78		»
classic toys	1K – 10K	Medium	CA$0.66		»
antique toys for sale	100 – 1K	High	CA$0.82		»
vintage toy store	1K – 10K	Medium	CA$0.60		»

there is a text box where you type the focus keyword for each page or post. Once identified, you want to ensure your keyword appears in key parts of your post including:

- Page title at the top of the webpage as a headline for the content
- Close to the beginning of your text, ideally in the first paragraph
- In level H1 or H2 headings in your copy
- The page's website address also known as the URL
- In one of the many tags that describe the content
- In the alt tags for images that are part of the content

- Repeated in the body text as many times as flows naturally

- In the meta description that appears as a preview in search results

It is essential to use your keyword frequently but not too frequently. You want to balance your keyword density without making it too dense. Search engines will penalize your content if it includes too many occurrences of the keyword. This is called keyword stuffing. In general, I advise that you include your keyword where it appears naturally in your copy and in the technical things noted above.

Search Engine Optimization is a specialized and ever-changing field. Keep up to date on the latest SEO methods through industry sources such as Search Engine Land or Social Media Examiner. Hire an experienced SEO consultant with a proven track record, if budgets permit.

3.2 Style guide

A style guide is a resource writers can access to settle certain matters of grammar, spelling, and other issues. Just as there are many different types of English, there are many different approaches to what is correct content. To create text consistent with a specific standard, pick a published style guide. Popular options include:

- *The Chicago Manual of Style*

- *The Microsoft Manual of Style*

- *The Associated Press Stylebook*

- *The Canadian Press Stylebook*

When creating content for a specific industry, consult the trade association or governing body. The industry may have its own style guide. For example, the American Chemical Society publishes *The ACS Style Guide.*

In addition to referring to a style guide, make your own. A simple text document can capture decisions made about style for your content creators. This will help you be consistent across all content with conventions you want to control. Your customized style guide can include:

- Conventions of capitalization for product names and job titles

- Frequently used trademarks and wordmarks

- Spelling of proper names including brands and employees

- Commonly used abbreviations, initialisms, and acronyms

Used together, a published style guide and customized style guide provide an essential resource for all your contributors from writers and editors, to videographers and closed captioning specialists. If everyone adheres to the style guide your content is more consistent, looks more professional, and reduces confusion.

3.3 Finding your voice

As you create content, you'll use your voice in every piece. Your voice might be informal, using casual phrases, slang, and informal structure. In contrast, your voice may be formal, drawing on more academic or business-oriented words. The voice should reflect your purpose and be comfortable and familiar for your audience.

I've seen many organizations try to dictate the voice their content creators use. The intent seems to be to control content to such an extent it appears to come from a single narrator. I assure you that successful companies allow their content creators to use many natural, overlapping voices. The collective contributions reflect the voice of the organization.

Content that echoes the voices of the creators themselves has more vibrancy and variety. Let your creators contribute in the tone they use in their everyday lives. Trying to mash everyone into a single tone of voice just creates a flat, uninteresting voice. Allow your content creators to be dynamic and interesting. The cadence of their words — in writing and out loud — is far more likely to engage your audience. Trust that you've hired the correct writers, podcasters, or videographers. If they are a match for your corporate culture, their voice is your voice.

4. Image Advice

When creating content, you have numerous options when it comes to images. Images can become stand-alone content pieces or they can appear with text, accompanying audio, or as part of videos. In broad terms, you can create photos or graphics.

In this section, I'm going to share advice to help you get started with each image type. There's lots of room for experimentation and creativity.

4.1 Use photos

When it comes to photos, you've got three main options. You can take your own. You can buy photos from a photographer or stock agency such as www.iStock.com. You can commission a photographer to create the photos you want. Each of these paths will help you create photos you can use legitimately. Don't steal images off the Internet!

Most importantly, the photos you use should tell a story. This may be directly related to the content topic you are creating or a supplement to the main point. The image should evoke an emotion.

If you take photographs yourself or work with a photographer, here are some points to consider:

- Think about what orientation will work best on your platform. Do you need portrait or landscape images?

- Square is essential for social sharing on Instagram. Can you crop the original picture to suit?

- Include white space in some of your photographs. This gives you the freedom to overlay type right on the picture as you create content. This can be a caption, a message, a credit.

- Color is also an important consideration. Do you want to present your content in full color or will you add a filter to adjust it? Maybe a vintage look in sepia or black and white would work best.

- Think also about the color in your image. Do you want a monotone palette focused on a single color or complementary colors like blue and orange playing against one another?

- Imagine each image as a grid three across by three high giving you nine squares with which to work. Best practice in photography has you explore the rule of thirds. Perhaps your subject takes up just one third of the image?

- The composition of each image is important. Use the rule of thirds to plan out close-up shots and action shots. Consider different angles beyond straight ahead. Get down low, or up high, or off to the side to see how that changes the photo.

- Lighting is crucial to great photographs. Give your camera something to work with! The better the light the more detail you'll capture in your photo. Be alert to glare from direct sunlight and lamps. Glare may suit your content style, or be something to avoid!

- Select your background with care. It should add to the story you are telling in the photo. Also be alert to unflattering things growing out of the top of people's heads. No human needs antennae.

- Be aware of text on buildings and objects in photos. Are you infringing on someone's copyright? Will a global audience understand them? Place names translate well but other words may cause confusion or, potentially, offense.

If you are taking your own photographs, capture images everywhere you go. Use the best camera you have on you at the time. Today's mobile phones have great cameras built in.

If you are working with a professional photographer, give her clear information about what you're hoping to achieve and step back to give her the freedom to create for you.

With these tips in mind, you can begin to capture the photographs you need for your content plan.

4.2 Use graphics

Graphics can include illustrations, technical drawings, infographics, charts, and any other visual part of the content you create. Similar to photographs, you can draw, buy, or commission custom graphics.

Focus on a single purpose in each graphic. If you have more than one thing to communicate, build another graphic.

When building graphics, readability is crucial. Select readable fonts and line lengths. Think about your platform and how your audience will consume the information. A giant, text-heavy graphic is hard to read on a mobile device, for example.

Illustrations can include anything from original artwork used with the artist's permission to custom drawings visualizing a content topic.

In some work environments, technical drawings are vital as you communicate information about a machine or process. Often you can access technical drawings from the design or engineering department. Be prepared to adapt the drawings to suit your audience.

Infographics are a specialized graphic that visually communicates a data set. Often, survey results are conveyed in this way so that the facts and figures are easier to understand.

While they may seem mundane to some content creators, charts and graphs are useful visuals for many topics. If colleagues are working in word processing or spreadsheet programs, data can be easily rendered as a chart or graph to illustrate your content piece.

As you create images, keep in mind the different formats needed for various promotional channels, especially social media. It's much easier to create a square variation of a graphic at the same time you create the version that will go in your content.

With these tips in mind, you can begin to create the graphics you need for your content plan.

5. Recording Audio

Audio recording does not have to be an expensive proposition. With the portable gear and software available today, you can readily create an environment to record quality podcasts in your home or office. Keep it simple. All you really need is a quality microphone, a computer, editing software, an Internet connection, and something to say.

5.1 Microphones

The quality of your audio recording starts with the quality of your microphone. No one enjoys listening to hiss and static and you risk losing listeners who can't stand poor audio. Invest in a high quality microphone but remember that cost is not the best indicator of quality. You can get great microphones for less than $100. Consider these things:

- Look for recommended brands including Sennheiser, Plantronics, Blue Electronics, and Audio Technica.

- Look for a dynamic microphone rather than a condenser microphone. Each records sound differently and, generally, dynamic is better for spoken word recordings.

- Consider how you'll be recording. An omnidirectional microphone captures a sphere of sound around the microphone, whereas, a cardioid microphone will pick up sound from a narrower area.

- Consider whether to invest in a microphone that connects via USB or 3.5 mm jack. Audiophiles disagree on which gives you better audio quality.

- If you breathe audibly, you need a buffer between you and the microphone. For about $10 you can eliminate this unwanted sound with a special piece of foam or mesh called a pop filter.

Before you purchase a microphone, ask around. It's likely you can borrow a microphone from a friend or colleague to try before you buy.

5.2 Recording location

Recording space also affects quality. I know people who record podcasts in their home office, around a dining table, in a standard office, in a boardroom, and in a sound-baffled supply closet. Use any space that works. In some situations, contributors will be in different places and you'll combine or balance all recordings at the editing stage.

Whatever space you use, do what you can to minimize background noise. This might include putting mobile phones in airplane mode, turning off unused equipment, and having only people involved in the recording in the space. Sound bounces off hard surfaces and can create echo or otherwise distort the audio captured. Bring in upholstered furniture and hang blankets over walls and windows. Consider investing in acoustic tiles to place around the room.

Once you're set up to record, there are some simple things you can do to improve the sound captured.

- Control your breathing. Don't pant, gasp, or sigh, if you can help it.

- Turn away from the microphone if you have to cough or sneeze.

- Take off jewelry that might bump the microphone.

- Remember that motion can be picked up on a microphone so don't thump the table for emphasis.

5.3 Audio editing

Content creators recording audio need editing software to refine and compile their audio recordings. Audacity and Adobe Audition are available for both Mac and PC. Audacity is free whereas Adobe Audition requires a monthly Adobe Creative Cloud membership. If you're a Mac user, another free option is Garage Band.

Whatever editing software you select, you'll compile the various audio components of your podcast. These might include:

- Theme song

- Opening remarks

- Content piece #1

- Sponsor recognition

- Content piece #2

- Paid advertisement

- Content piece #3

- Acknowledgments

- Concluding remarks

Using Audacity, Adobe Audition, Garage Band, or other software of choice, you'll splice all of your audio components into a single episode. You'll also have the opportunity to add transitions such as fade, overlap the beginnings and endings of selected segments, and balance sound levels. If necessary, you have the tools to alter speed of playback, adjust pitch and, to some extent, improve the audio quality.

As always, don't let the space, equipment, or software stop you from recording. Use whatever you have and plan to invest in better quality equipment, if needed. Or reach out to a podcaster whose sound quality you like and ask about his or her setup. Remember my earlier remarks about imperfect action. However you set yourself up to record audio, start simply and add additional resources as you expand your podcasting efforts.

6. Use Video

Current video options include recorded and live content. You can use content planning to determine what videos you will create. You also have the option to identify existing videos that you'll embed in your own content. Content planning strategies can also be used to identify and plan for livestreaming opportunities.

As you create video, keep in mind that this medium can include live action, scripted segments, animation, screencasting, and slide shows.

> Screencasting is the process of recording what appears on your computer's monitor as you execute a task. You can also record video of your mobile phone or tablet screen. This is a great tool to share technical how-tos and to show and tell Internet content. Typically, the screencast includes a voiceover audio track so viewers get a verbal description of what you're doing. To learn more about screencasting, I recommend Steve Dotto's online course Screencasting Made Easy at www.dottotech.com.

6.1 Make videos

Video can be as simple or complex as suits your content plan. You may start out with a single camera shot using your mobile phone or use the webcam on your computer. As you gain experience, you'll add additional tools such as a digital video camera, tripod, microphone, and professional lighting. You have many options when it comes to video cameras. Initially, you'll use whatever you have available whether that's a smartphone app or your current digital SLR camera. When you're ready to invest in a video camera consider the following:

- Can you handle the camera comfortably?

- Are the operating buttons accessible?

- Does the camera have removable or expandable memory?

- Are you recording in standard definition (SD), high definition (HD), or something else?

- What is the true resolution? Your video quality will be higher with a greater number of pixels.

- What file format is recorded?

- How does the camera perform in low light situations? Do you shoot in low light?

- Is there a zoom function?

- How good is the image stability?

- Is there a view screen? Can it be repositioned?

- What is the battery life? Can you buy extra batteries?

- What sort of connector does the camera use?

- What weather conditions can the camera handle? Do you need a waterproof solution?

- How much does it cost? Is this within your budget?

Visit any consumer electronics store or online retailer and you'll be overwhelmed with options. As with microphones, ask around to see what other people are using. Ask for a demonstration, if possible. Publicist and podcaster Kimberly Plumley recommends the Zoom Q8 video and audio recorder. It's a compact but powerful camera that records high definition video and up to four channels of audio.

In some cases, you'll share raw footage just as it appears on your camera. Other times you'll incorporate graphics, music, voiceovers, and closed captioning. You may also prepare animations or screencasts to include in your video content.

Video-focused content creators often work with a video editor to mix together a variety of clips into a single video. Different camera angles, product shots, locations, and other video content elements can all be blended into a single video. In addition, you have the option to add a theme song, background music, graphic slides, and visual effects.

Video editing is a specialized skill and, like text editors, I recommend you hire a professional editor if your budget permits. Of course, there are robust, do-it-yourself, software packages available including CyberLink Power Director, Adobe Premiere Elements and Nero Video. In addition, YouTube offers a free video editor at www.youtube.com/editor. Using video editing software, you will be able to:

- Add video and audio clips

- Add photos

- Add music

- Insert transitions

- Include titles

- Code closed captions

- Compile a complete video

Once you've compiled your video, your content is ready to share with your audience.

6.2 Live streaming

Live streaming is one of the latest trends in social media. It involves broadcasting via a live streaming app anywhere with an Internet connection. Live streamers are sharing everything from retail shopping mall tours to nature walks by the river. It's an exciting medium because it happens in real time. Unexpected moments both good and bad appear in your video. Honest reactions and spontaneous enthusiasm are captured alongside humorous blunders. Live streaming gives the audience all of the raw content without filters or edits. In Chapter 4, I mentioned live streaming video tools including Facebook Live, Periscope, Twitch, Busker and UStream. With a smartphone app and Internet connection, content creators can use any or all of these services to live stream. In a content plan, you can plan for live streaming content in terms of topic, place and time. What ends up on camera depends on what happens.

In most cases, an archived copy of your live stream video is available for your audience to watch at a later date. If they missed the live broadcast, they can still experience your content. You can also download a copy of your video to edit clips to include in future video content plans.

If you haven't experienced live streaming yet, check out Ms. Candy Blog at www.mscandyblog.com. She regularly live streams about makeup, fashion, and candy on Facebook Live, Periscope, and Busker. She's a great role model for the raw enthusiasm a live stream content creator can bring to videos.

7. Legal Considerations

For every content format, there are legal considerations to keep in mind. As you build your content, you'll want to be aware of these issues to avoid future legal troubles. In particular, we're going to explore copyright, creative commons, and model releases. These legal considerations are the most common issues for content creators.

In this book, I provide some general information about common legal issues. This information is not intended to replace legal opinion. Please seek the advice of a qualified lawyer in your area, if needed.

7.1 Copyright

Copyright is the law that governs written works, images, performances, computer software, and some other types of intellectual property. In some cases, intellectual property is protected by patent law, trademark law, or another law. Copyright material can take many forms including the text, images, audio, and video you create in your content.

Careless content creators can be at risk of plagiarism if they use another person's text, images, audio, or video without permission. You must respect copyright for the integrity of your brand. Don't steal, copy, or reproduce photographs that aren't yours! This is copyright infringement.

Copyright is valid in most countries around the world through the Berne Copyright Convention, Universal Copyright Convention, Rome Convention, and the World Trade Organization. Copyright protects a specific expression of an idea. It does not protect the idea itself.

The length of time a copyright is valid varies. In the US, copyright duration is the life of the content creator plus an additional 70 years after death. In Canada, copyright duration is the life of the content creator plus 50 years, ending on December 31 of that year. If the content is a collaboration, the law applies to the life span of the last surviving contributor.

Works that are no longer under copyright are in the public domain and can be used by content creators. Materials may enter the public domain when the copyright expires. Alternatively, the content creator can declare his or her work to be in the public domain during his or her lifetime.

A trademark is another legal form of intellectual property. The trademark holder must secure the trademark in each country in which he or she operates. Once verified, he or she must invest resources to protect the copyright. You can use a trademark in your content as long as you acknowledge the trademark. Typically this is done in writing with the ™ symbol. Use of a trademark must not imply an endorsement, unless that formal relationship exists.

If you want to use copyrighted material, you must obtain permission from the copyright holder. The copyright holder may request a fee, grant a license for a period of time, or give permission freely. Seek permission by contacting the copyright owner, requesting permission, negotiating the terms, and documenting any agreement in writing.

While some content creators are tempted to ignore copyright, it's best to seek permission. For further information about copyright, visit www.copyright.gov in the US and www.accesscopyright.ca in Canada.

7.2 Creative commons

Creative commons is an alternative to copyright where content creators can give permission for their work to be used. This is not a blanket permission but rather permission as long as one or more conditions are followed. This can include attribution, noncommercial, no derivative works, and share alike. Sometimes two or more conditions apply.

The attribution condition requires the user to acknowledge the creator of the work being used. For example, a web page might include a photograph. Under a creative commons attribution agreement, the photographer would be credited by name in a caption.

The noncommercial condition allows the content creator to use the work if the content you create is not for sale. Generally this applies to private and nonprofit use. For example, a student musician might use part of a band's song in a new song, but the new song couldn't be sold.

The no derivative works condition grants permission for the work to be used in its entirety. So a set designer could incorporate an artist's painting on stage but the painting must be identical to the original.

The share alike condition requires that any new work created from the shared content be made available under a creative commons license.

Some creative common licenses apply more than one condition and you may want to use work that requires both attribution and the share alike condition. You also have the option to approach the original creator for permission to use the work beyond the creative commons license.

Platforms such as the photo sharing site Flickr and the video community YouTube are among the places you'll find content available under creative commons licenses. For more information about creative commons visit www.creativecommons.org.

7.3 Model release

If your content creation plans include images, quotes, or recordings of people then you may need a model release. Your participants have to understand that their voices, likenesses, and/or commentary will be published and they must agree to be in your content.

SAMPLE 9: RELEASE FORM

Release Form

Your Company
Name@YourCompany.com
(555) 555-5555
Date: _____

PHOTOGRAPHIC / AUDIO / VIDEO / TESTIMONIAL RELEASE

I, the undersigned, agree to bestow upon YOUR COMPANY the right to use recordings of me, both voice and likeness (hereinafter the "Recordings"), the right to use any written or verbal testimonials made by me (hereinafter the "Testimonials"), and the right to use any photographs of me for any of YOUR COMPANY'S websites, blogs, podcasts, videos, email newsletters, social media channels, workshops, public speaking engagements, and similar uses.

I understand and agree that YOUR COMPANY shall have the right to edit or abridge the Recordings, Testimonials, and/or photographs in whole or in part. I agree that YOUR COMPANY will exclusively own all of the footage of my appearance and participation in the program, and that YOUR COMPANY shall be entitled to edit and distribute the footage in its sole discretion, as it may deem appropriate.

I have not requested, and will not request neither now nor in the future, remuneration of any kind for the rights that I have assigned to YOUR COMPANY. YOUR COMPANY shall hold these rights in perpetuity.

I further consent to the reproduction and/or authorization by YOUR COMPANY to reproduce, sell, and use said photographs and recordings of my voice, for use in all domestic and foreign markets. Further, I understand that others, with or without the consent of YOUR COMPANY may use and/or reproduce such photographs and recordings.

I agree to indemnify and hold YOUR COMPANY harmless from and against all claims, demands, loss, liability, costs, damages, and expenses in connection with the Recordings or their broadcast, and in connection with the Testimonials and photographs or their publication.

I hereby release YOUR COMPANY and any of its associated or affiliated companies, their directors, officers, agents, employees, and customers, and appointed advertising agencies, their directors, officers, agents, and employees from all claims of every kind on account of such use.

You may withdraw from this session at any time. If you have any questions, you may ask now or at any time.

This is the entire agreement between us.

If you agree with these terms, please indicate your agreement by signing below.

If participant is under the age of majority, I, _____ as the parent/legal guardian of the individual named below, have read this release and approve of its terms.

Print Participant Name: _____
Signature: _____ (of Participant, or Guardian named above)
Print Witness Name: _____
Witness Address: _____
_____
_____
Witness Phone number: _____
Witness Signature: _____

[A second copy of this document has been provided for your records.]

Some situations will not require a release. Comments made at a press conference or public comments from a spokesperson or public figure are examples.

Extra care must be taken with regards to content featuring children or teens. While a child may be willing to participate, you need consent from a parent or guardian.

Working with a professional videographer or photographer and professional models or actors will take care of this requirement for you. By hiring them, you are paying for them to be in your content.

The generic release form in Sample 9 covers a wide range of formats and uses. You can adapt this document to your situation.

8. Publish to Your Platform

Once you've created your content and taken care of any legal details, you're almost ready to share that content with your audience.

8.1 Finalize content

Just prior to publication, it's time to check over your content one last time. In the appendix, you'll find a content creation checklist for each month. At this time, pause and make sure your content piece is complete.

The numbered rows represent the days of the month. Work across the row that matches your publication date. Working from left to right across the checklist, consider the following:

- Is the title correct? Does it include keywords?

- Have you acknowledged the author and other contributors?

- Have your keywords been inserted in the title, body copy, URL, tags, meta data, and so on?

- Have you assigned the content to a category?

- Have you tagged your content? Have you included hashtags, if appropriate to your platform?

- Are your images correct? Are they displaying with the correct aspect ratio? Did you include alternate text for the visually impaired?

- Have you uploaded the correct audio files? Does the media player work?

- Have you embedded your video files? Have you included closed captions?

SAMPLE 10: CREATION CHECKLIST

January Creation Checklist

Pub date	Scheduled	Title	Author	Keywords	Category	Tags	Image	Audio	Video	Links	SEO	Deliverable
1												
2	✓	Title A	Sc	cat	✓	✓	✓	✓		✓	✓	MP3
3												
4	✓	Title B	BR	plane	✓	✓	✓		✓	✓	✓	ebook
5												
6												
7												
8												
9												
10												
11												
12												
13												
14												
15												
16	✓	Title C	Sc	dog	✓	✓	✓			✓	✓	none
17												
18	✓	Title D	BR	car	✓	✓	✓				✓	PDF
19												
20												
21												
22												
23												
24												
25												
26												
27												
28												
29												
30	✓	Title E	Sc	snake	✓	✓	✓		✓	✓	✓	ebook
31												

- Do the links work? Should you be using any affiliate links? Have you disclosed your affiliates?

- Have you done all you can to optimize SEO?

- Is your email opt-in/unsubscribe system working correctly?

8.2 Approvals

As we discussed during Chapter 6, Step 5: Make an Editorial Calendar, your content may be subject to approvals from management, your client, or a business partner. Before you publish your content ensure you have all the necessary approvals in place.

Some teams use an informal approval process. It can be as casual as a thumbs up between cubicles. Other organizations have a content review meeting where content approval is documented in the minutes. Still others use a digital approval system to sign off on content. In rare cases, a more formal sign-off document is necessary.

Make your approval process as simple as possible. The simpler the approval process the easier it will be to publish great content!

8.3 Publish now versus schedule for later

There are two options when content is ready to be published. It can be published right away or scheduled for a later time. There are pros and cons to either method. You choose the method that works for you.

Your platform may dictate if you can schedule content for a later time. Not all publishing tools allow you to privately upload complete and approved content. If this is your situation, you have no choice but to publish right away.

However, most tools do have a schedule feature and you get to pick the date of publication. You can schedule when web pages, blog posts, email newsletters, and other formats go public. The scheduled date should match the publication date outlined in your editorial calendar.

It's possible to share content as soon it's ready. If your information is time sensitive, you'll want to share it as soon as possible. However, will your content be as effective published in the moment?

The reason you create a content plan is to ensure your work is fully supported. Up to this stage, you've followed all the steps in the cycle. If you publish right away, are you prepared to share and monitor the reaction? Are you ready to gather the statistics that will help you evaluate your content's success and make improvements? I talk more about both these tasks in Chapter 8, Step 7: Share, Monitor, and Evaluate.

8

Step 7:
Share, Monitor, and Evaluate

1. Share

Once you've created and published your content, it's time to let the world know about your new work. Be proud of your new content and share it everywhere you can. You've got to take the initiative as this is not a "build it and they will come" situation. You've got to build it and then spread your idea around with enthusiasm.

1.1 Start with your true fans

True fans are your biggest champions! True fans believe in your products and ideas. They advocate for your work and are most likely to interact with new content. They enjoy being part of your inner circle and are among the first to know what's new with you.

Whatever your platform, your true fans will be among the first people to learn about each new piece of content. They are likely subscribed to your RSS feed, podcast, or email newsletter. They may belong to one of your Facebook groups. They may get a social notification, automatic download, or new content email. However they find your new content, they will be excited to read, listen, or watch.

Even if your primary platform is a website or blog, you can still develop an email list to connect with fans. This is a sound business strategy to keep in touch with your true fans. If an email newsletter is not your primary platform, you can still create a newsletter as a secondary platform. Emails you send can include links to your content on other platforms.

Don't forget to include your colleagues at the office as true fans. Often content creation is done by a communication department somewhat separated from the rest of the organization. Let everyone know about new content as it's published.

1.2 Make the most of social media

Social media is one of the most effective ways to share new content. Whether you prefer Facebook or Snapchat or something else, there's always an opportunity to share.

Success with social media requires you (or your brand) to be present and interact with friends or followers on an ongoing basis. Successful social campaigns involve interaction. Talk to your friends and followers to cultivate relationships. Over time, they may join your crew of true fans.

This book is not a tutorial on social media sharing, but I do want to remind you of some of the key social media channels available to you. Often you can use each social network in more than one way. While these will evolve over time, these include but are not limited to:

- **Facebook:** This offers opportunities through profiles, pages and groups. Use your personal profile or corporate page to share links to your content. If you're interacting with people interested in your subject, share links in relevant groups. Be sure to share to be informative not self-promotional! You also have the option to do Facebook Live video to talk about your content.

- **Instagram posts and Instagram Stories:** These offer great ways to share images and short videos. Remember to use the images cropped to square and shoot video in vertical mode. Hashtags are big on Instagram to help you share with a wider audience.

- **Twitter:** Tweet your link on Twitter to spread the word. For more engagement, "@ mention" contributors or key thinkers in your topic area. Again, you can use hashtags to grow your audience.

- **LinkedIn:** This is the place to share with the business community. You can post an update to your individual or corporate profile. Make use of LinkedIn Pulse, too, if your text-based content is appropriate to the LinkedIn community.

- **Pinterest:** This is the community for do-it-yourselfers and researchers. If you've got images in your content, create a Pinterest Board to highlight your work. Look for themes across all your content to select board topics that can be continually refreshed with new content.

- **YouTube:** If you have a YouTube channel, use it as a social network. Respond to comments.

This list represents only a few of your options when it comes to social media. Reflect back on the work you did in Step 2 to learn about your audience. Where do they hang out online? Are they using MySpace? If they are, you should, too. Be alert to changes in the social media scene. A year ago Instagram Stories did not exist. Who knows what will be available a year in the future?

1.3 Get out in the world

Content sharing happens offline as well as online. Perhaps your content creator or company spokesperson does regular public appearances. When it is natural to do so, he or she has the opportunity to invite his or her audience to engage with your content.

Educational settings are another great way to share your content. Perhaps someone on your team is a college lecturer. If your subject supports academic pursuits, cultivate relationships with professors, lecturers, sessional instructors, and teaching assistants armed with the latest content; they can share up-to-date information with students.

Similarly, professional development settings can be another great place to share your content. Someone from your content creation team with public speaking skills can offer a lunch-and-learn session to local business groups, academic groups, or hobbyists enthusiastic about your topic. The presentation could include highlights of the content you've created. Attendees can be provided with links to the content itself for further information.

Events are an underutilized way to share content. Don't be the cheesy networker talking exclusively about your project. You've got to join conversations in a genuine way. If you meet people interested in your topic, you may have the opportunity to invite people to read/listen/watch.

Don't forget traditional media. Magazines, radio, and television are all looking for great content. When you have a significant piece of content, you have the option to promote it yourself or with the help of a publicist. A press release may just get you a media appearance to reach your audience in a new way.

Trade shows are another great place to share your content. Company experts in the booth will talk with conference goers about your organization's purpose. You can even use content you've created in the booth design. Share photographs on the backdrop, include video projection, and distribute print or digital copies of content. Share swag that includes a link to find your content.

Attend as many conferences as you can. Share what you know. Learn from others. Look for speaking opportunities and engage both speakers and attendees in conversation. But apply to be a speaker from a place of service, not salesy promotion.

To help you keep track of your sharing efforts, the workbook in the appendix (and on the download kit) includes a monthly promotional checklist. As you share your content in one of the ways listed, check off that square. The checklist includes blank columns for you to add your custom promotion efforts.

2. Monitor

Once shared, your next task is to monitor the response. You've got to be prepared to interact with your audience. You've included time for this in your editorial calendar and I encourage you to use it.

2.1 Respond and interact

Let your audience know you see or hear them. The first step to successful engagement is to acknowledge their presence. Answer their questions, engage them in conversation, and provide links to related content of interest. Those links should include your work and other content creators' efforts. Frequently thank your audience for their interest and support.

2.2 Reward true fans

As you monitor your content for responses, be alert for your true fans. Give them a special shout-out, if you can. On occasion, offer true fans special perks such as a true-fans-only digital or live event. Do everything you can to support and appreciate your true fans. They are influencers who can share their enthusiasm for your work with a wider audience. Brand advocates must be treasured!

SAMPLE 11: PROMOTION CHECKLIST

January Promotion Checklist

Pub Date	True Fans	Internal	Facebook	Instagram	Twitter	LinkedIn	SnapChat	Pinterest	YouTube	Appearances	Events	Publicity	Periscope						
1																			
2	✓	✓	✓	✓	✓			✓	✓		✓		✓						
3																			
4	✓	✓		✓	✓	✓				✓									
5																			
6																			
7																			
8																			
9																			
10																			
11																			
12																			
13																			
14																			
15																			
16	✓	✓	✓	✓	✓			✓	✓		✓	✓							
17																			
18	✓		✓	✓	✓	✓				✓									
19																			
20																			
21																			
22																			
23																			
24																			
25																			
26																			
27																			
28																			
29																			
30	✓	✓	✓	✓	✓			✓	✓		✓	✓							
31																			

2.3 Dealing with negativity

On occasion, you may publish content that receives a negative reaction. Dealing with negativity requires tact and diplomacy. Step back and take a breath. Don't respond from a place of anger or frustration.

It's possible you've made a factual error that's resulted in the negative comment. If so, acknowledge the error and correct it. You can edit the original content or add an addendum apologizing for the mistake and offering the correct details. Sometimes the "right" answer is a matter of opinion. You're entitled to your opinion but it's respectful to acknowledge another point of view.

If your negative comments are vicious personal attacks or threatening in any way, you're probably dealing with an Internet troll. Trolls are best ignored. Do take a moment to document the information as a screen capture. If the situation ever escalates, you'll have evidence to demonstrate a pattern of behavior.

Some content creators will deal with negativity by deleting comments, banning followers, and blocking fans. It's a good idea to have a policy about how your organization will deal with negativity.

3. Evaluate

Everything in online content can be measured. Metrics provide detailed information about how and when people are consuming your content. As you decide which metrics to focus on, think back to your purpose.

Are you trying to grow an audience? Then look at growth in fans and followers. Are you hoping to improve engagement? Then review the number and quality of your interactions. Are you driven by sales? Then analyze your sales funnel.

The appendix includes goal tracking worksheets. Use the blank columns to add custom metrics. Fill in the tracking data monthly to chart your progress.

- **Website or blog**
  - Page views
  - Bounce rate
  - Unique visitors
  - Progress through the sales funnel

- **Podcast**
  - Total subscribers
  - New subscribers and unsubscribes
  - Downloads
- **Video**
  - Total subscribers
  - New subscribers and unsubscribes
  - Views
- **Newsletter**
  - Total Subscribers
  - New subscribers and unsubscribes
  - Opens
  - Clicks
  - Delivery performance
- **Social media**
  - Total fans or followers
  - Tally of likes
  - Summary of comments
  - Volume of interactions
  - Number of meaningful dialogues

3.1 Interpret the data

Once you've gathered your numbers, the analysis can show you trends. Is your audience growing? Are your engagements decreasing? Can you correlate sales to website traffic?

With consistent content planning efforts you can grow your success, however it's defined.

Conclusion

Congratulations! You've completed your first content planning cycle. I trust *The Content Planner* has provided you with a framework to create great content in service of your community. As Karine Bengualid said, "Content is kind of a big deal."

With a strong purpose in mind, you've gotten better acquainted with your audience and figured out where to connect with them. You've used brainstorming and research to identify content ideas and put the best of them on your editorial calendar. And you've explored how to create strong text, images, audio, and video to share with your audience. Add to that your efforts to evaluate the results and make better plans for the next cycle and you've made a Herculean effort. Bravo!

Don't forget that additional copies of the workbook in the appendix are available on the download kit included with this book.

Content creation requires dedication. I encourage you to make content creation a habit. Look for content opportunities every day and do your best to create meaningful, useful, interesting content that adds to the online dialogue. Your community will grow if you can serve them a steady diet of great content.

I'd love to read, watch, and listen to the content you're creating. Tag @AngelaCrocker in a tweet or on Instagram to show me what you're up to. Or visit me at my personal website, www.AngelaCrocker.com, to connect other ways. I wish you every success!

Appendix:
Content Planner Workbook

This workbook is a companion to *The Content Planner: A Complete Guide to Organize and Share Your Ideas Online. The Content Planner* cycle walks you through seven steps to help you build your content plan. The method is suitable for websites, blogs, podcasts, video, email newsletters, and even, social networks.

As you work to create your content plan, use these worksheets to capture your ideas and organize your work. If you need more blank copies, print your own from the digital download kit included with your book.

1. Worksheets

Purpose Statement Worksheet

Check all that apply:

☐ Marketing and promotion   ☐ Sales

☐ Differentiate brand   ☐ Credibility

☐ Customer service   ☐ Grow audience

☐ Market research   ☐ Support partners

☐ Portfolio   ☐ Others: _____

Purpose Statement

SMART goals to support the purpose statement:

1. _____

_____

2. _____

_____

3. _____

_____

Notes:

Persona Worksheet

```
┌─────────────────┐
│                 │     Demographics:
│                 │
│     Place       │     Age: _____      Location: _____
│     Photo       │     Marital Status: _____   Gender: _____
│     Here        │     Children: _____     Nationality: _____
│                 │     Height: _____      Heritage: _____
│                 │     Weight: _____       Other: _____
└─────────────────┘
```

Name: _____

Education	Economics
Career	Shopping
Politics	Fitness
Religion	Home
Medical	History

Platform Worksheet

Primary location

Secondary locations

- ☐ Website ☐ Video channel
- ☐ Blog ☐ email newsletters
- ☐ Podcast ☐ Other _____

☐ Online communities

- • _____
- • _____
- • _____
- • _____

☐ News sites

- • _____
- • _____
- • _____
- • _____

☐ Social networks

- ☐ Facebook ☐ LinkedIn
- ☐ Twitter ☐ Snapchat
- ☐ Instagram ☐ Others _____

Notes:

Goal Tracking Worksheet: Website or blog

	Page views	Bounce rate	Unique visitors	Sales funnel			
January							
February							
March							
April							
May							
June							
July							
August							
September							
October							
November							
December							

Notes:

Goal Tracking Worksheet: Podcast

	Total subscribers	New subscribers	Unsubscribes	Downloads		
January						
February						
March						
April						
May						
June						
July						
August						
September						
October						
November						
December						

Notes:

Goal Tracking Worksheet: Video

	Total subscribers	New subscribers	Unsubscribes	Views		
January						
February						
March						
April						
May						
June						
July						
August						
September						
October						
November						
December						

Notes:

Goal Tracking Worksheet: Newsletter

	Total subscribers	New subscribers	Unsubscribes	Opens	Clicks	Delivery performance	
January							
February							
March							
April							
May							
June							
July							
August							
September							
October							
November							
December							

Notes:

Goal Tracking Worksheet: Social media

	Total fans or followers	Tally of likes	Summary of comments	Volume of interactions	Number of meaningful dialogues		
January							
February							
March							
April							
May							
June							
July							
August							
September							
October							
November							
December							

Notes:

Goal Tracking Worksheet: Other

January						
February						
March						
April						
May						
June						
July						
August						
September						
October						
November						
December						

Notes:

2. Monthly Calendars for Planning and Tracking

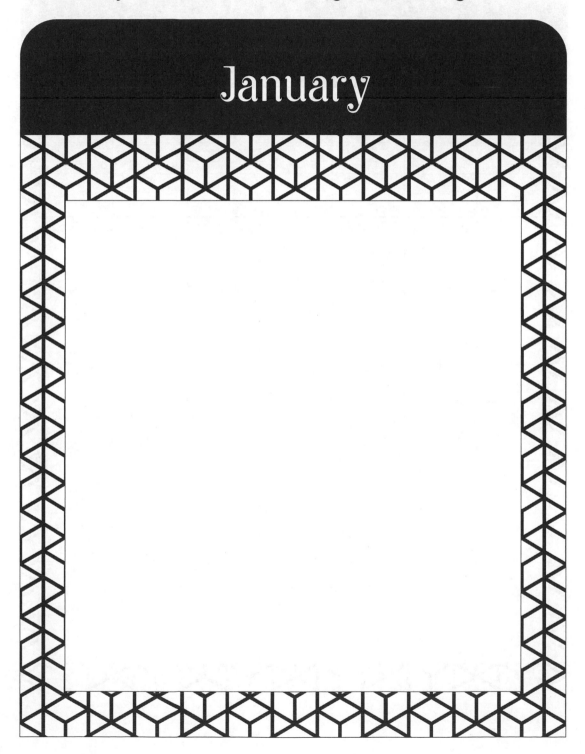

January

January

Sunday	Monday	Tuesday	Wednesday	Thursday	Friday	Saturday

Notes:

January Creation Checklist

Pub date	Scheduled	Title	Author	Keywords	Category	Tags	Image	Audio	Video	Links	SEO	Deliverable
1												
2												
3												
4												
5												
6												
7												
8												
9												
10												
11												
12												
13												
14												
15												
16												
17												
18												
19												
20												
21												
22												
23												
24												
25												
26												
27												
28												
29												
30												
31												

January Promotion Checklist

Pub Date	True Fans	Internal	Facebook	Instagram	Twitter	LinkedIn	SnapChat	Pinterest	YouTube	Appearances	Events	Publicity								
1																				
2																				
3																				
4																				
5																				
6																				
7																				
8																				
9																				
10																				
11																				
12																				
13																				
14																				
15																				
16																				
17																				
18																				
19																				
20																				
21																				
22																				
23																				
24																				
25																				
26																				
27																				
28																				
29																				
30																				
31																				

February

February

Sunday	Monday	Tuesday	Wednesday	Thursday	Friday	Saturday

Notes:

February Creation Checklist

Pub date	Scheduled	Title	Author	Keywords	Category	Tags	Image	Audio	Video	Links	SEO	Deliverable
1												
2												
3												
4												
5												
6												
7												
8												
9												
10												
11												
12												
13												
14												
15												
16												
17												
18												
19												
20												
21												
22												
23												
24												
25												
26												
27												
28												
29												

February Promotion Checklist

Pub Date	True Fans	Internal	Facebook	Instagram	Twitter	LinkedIn	SnapChat	Pinterest	YouTube	Appearances	Events	Publicity								
1																				
2																				
3																				
4																				
5																				
6																				
7																				
8																				
9																				
10																				
11																				
12																				
13																				
14																				
15																				
16																				
17																				
18																				
19																				
20																				
21																				
22																				
23																				
24																				
25																				
26																				
27																				
28																				
29																				

March

March

Sunday	Monday	Tuesday	Wednesday	Thursday	Friday	Saturday

Notes:

March Creation Checklist

Pub date	Scheduled	Title	Author	Keywords	Category	Tags	Image	Audio	Video	Links	SEO	Deliverable
1												
2												
3												
4												
5												
6												
7												
8												
9												
10												
11												
12												
13												
14												
15												
16												
17												
18												
19												
20												
21												
22												
23												
24												
25												
26												
27												
28												
29												
30												
31												

March Promotion Checklist

Pub Date	True Fans	Internal	Facebook	Instagram	Twitter	LinkedIn	SnapChat	Pinterest	YouTube	Appearances	Events	Publicity							
1																			
2																			
3																			
4																			
5																			
6																			
7																			
8																			
9																			
10																			
11																			
12																			
13																			
14																			
15																			
16																			
17																			
18																			
19																			
20																			
21																			
22																			
23																			
24																			
25																			
26																			
27																			
28																			
29																			
30																			
31																			

April

April

Sunday	Monday	Tuesday	Wednesday	Thursday	Friday	Saturday

Notes:

April Creation Checklist

Pub date	Scheduled	Title	Author	Keywords	Category	Tags	Image	Audio	Video	Links	SEO	Deliverable
1												
2												
3												
4												
5												
6												
7												
8												
9												
10												
11												
12												
13												
14												
15												
16												
17												
18												
19												
20												
21												
22												
23												
24												
25												
26												
27												
28												
29												
30												

April Promotion Checklist

Pub Date	True Fans	Internal	Facebook	Instagram	Twitter	LinkedIn	SnapChat	Pinterest	YouTube	Appearances	Events	Publicity								
1																				
2																				
3																				
4																				
5																				
6																				
7																				
8																				
9																				
10																				
11																				
12																				
13																				
14																				
15																				
16																				
17																				
18																				
19																				
20																				
21																				
22																				
23																				
24																				
25																				
26																				
27																				
28																				
29																				
30																				

May

May

Sunday	Monday	Tuesday	Wednesday	Thursday	Friday	Saturday

Notes:

May Creation Checklist

Pub date	Scheduled	Title	Author	Keywords	Category	Tags	Image	Audio	Video	Links	SEO	Deliverable
1												
2												
3												
4												
5												
6												
7												
8												
9												
10												
11												
12												
13												
14												
15												
16												
17												
18												
19												
20												
21												
22												
23												
24												
25												
26												
27												
28												
29												
30												
31												

May Promotion Checklist

Pub Date	True Fans	Internal	Facebook	Instagram	Twitter	LinkedIn	SnapChat	Pinterest	YouTube	Appearances	Events	Publicity							
1																			
2																			
3																			
4																			
5																			
6																			
7																			
8																			
9																			
10																			
11																			
12																			
13																			
14																			
15																			
16																			
17																			
18																			
19																			
20																			
21																			
22																			
23																			
24																			
25																			
26																			
27																			
28																			
29																			
30																			
31																			

June

June

Sunday	Monday	Tuesday	Wednesday	Thursday	Friday	Saturday

Notes:

June Creation Checklist

Pub date	Scheduled	Title	Author	Keywords	Category	Tags	Image	Audio	Video	Links	SEO	Deliverable
1												
2												
3												
4												
5												
6												
7												
8												
9												
10												
11												
12												
13												
14												
15												
16												
17												
18												
19												
20												
21												
22												
23												
24												
25												
26												
27												
28												
29												
30												

June Promotion Checklist

Pub Date	True Fans	Internal	Facebook	Instagram	Twitter	LinkedIn	SnapChat	Pinterest	YouTube	Appearances	Events	Publicity							
1																			
2																			
3																			
4																			
5																			
6																			
7																			
8																			
9																			
10																			
11																			
12																			
13																			
14																			
15																			
16																			
17																			
18																			
19																			
20																			
21																			
22																			
23																			
24																			
25																			
26																			
27																			
28																			
29																			
30																			

July

July

Sunday	Monday	Tuesday	Wednesday	Thursday	Friday	Saturday

Notes:

July Creation Checklist

Pub date	Scheduled	Title	Author	Keywords	Category	Tags	Image	Audio	Video	Links	SEO	Deliverable
1												
2												
3												
4												
5												
6												
7												
8												
9												
10												
11												
12												
13												
14												
15												
16												
17												
18												
19												
20												
21												
22												
23												
24												
25												
26												
27												
28												
29												
30												
31												

July Promotion Checklist

Pub Date	True Fans	Internal	Facebook	Instagram	Twitter	LinkedIn	SnapChat	Pinterest	YouTube	Appearances	Events	Publicity							
1																			
2																			
3																			
4																			
5																			
6																			
7																			
8																			
9																			
10																			
11																			
12																			
13																			
14																			
15																			
16																			
17																			
18																			
19																			
20																			
21																			
22																			
23																			
24																			
25																			
26																			
27																			
28																			
29																			
30																			
31																			

August

August

Sunday	Monday	Tuesday	Wednesday	Thursday	Friday	Saturday

Notes:

August Creation Checklist

Pub date	Scheduled	Title	Author	Keywords	Category	Tags	Image	Audio	Video	Links	SEO	Deliverable
1												
2												
3												
4												
5												
6												
7												
8												
9												
10												
11												
12												
13												
14												
15												
16												
17												
18												
19												
20												
21												
22												
23												
24												
25												
26												
27												
28												
29												
30												
31												

August Promotion Checklist

Pub Date	True Fans	Internal	Facebook	Instagram	Twitter	LinkedIn	SnapChat	Pinterest	YouTube	Appearances	Events	Publicity						
1																		
2																		
3																		
4																		
5																		
6																		
7																		
8																		
9																		
10																		
11																		
12																		
13																		
14																		
15																		
16																		
17																		
18																		
19																		
20																		
21																		
22																		
23																		
24																		
25																		
26																		
27																		
28																		
29																		
30																		
31																		

September

September

Sunday	Monday	Tuesday	Wednesday	Thursday	Friday	Saturday

Notes:

September Creation Checklist

Pub date	Scheduled	Title	Author	Keywords	Category	Tags	Image	Audio	Video	Links	SEO	Deliverable
1												
2												
3												
4												
5												
6												
7												
8												
9												
10												
11												
12												
13												
14												
15												
16												
17												
18												
19												
20												
21												
22												
23												
24												
25												
26												
27												
28												
29												
30												

September Promotion Checklist

Pub Date	True Fans	Internal	Facebook	Instagram	Twitter	LinkedIn	SnapChat	Pinterest	YouTube	Appearances	Events	Publicity								
1																				
2																				
3																				
4																				
5																				
6																				
7																				
8																				
9																				
10																				
11																				
12																				
13																				
14																				
15																				
16																				
17																				
18																				
19																				
20																				
21																				
22																				
23																				
24																				
25																				
26																				
27																				
28																				
29																				
30																				

October

October

Sunday	Monday	Tuesday	Wednesday	Thursday	Friday	Saturday

Notes:

October Creation Checklist

Pub date	Scheduled	Title	Author	Keywords	Category	Tags	Image	Audio	Video	Links	SEO	Deliverable
1												
2												
3												
4												
5												
6												
7												
8												
9												
10												
11												
12												
13												
14												
15												
16												
17												
18												
19												
20												
21												
22												
23												
24												
25												
26												
27												
28												
29												
30												
31												

October Promotion Checklist

Pub Date	True Fans	Internal	Facebook	Instagram	Twitter	LinkedIn	SnapChat	Pinterest	YouTube	Appearances	Events	Publicity								
1																				
2																				
3																				
4																				
5																				
6																				
7																				
8																				
9																				
10																				
11																				
12																				
13																				
14																				
15																				
16																				
17																				
18																				
19																				
20																				
21																				
22																				
23																				
24																				
25																				
26																				
27																				
28																				
29																				
30																				
31																				

November

November

Sunday	Monday	Tuesday	Wednesday	Thursday	Friday	Saturday

Notes:

November Creation Checklist

Pub date	Scheduled	Title	Author	Keywords	Category	Tags	Image	Audio	Video	Links	SEO	Deliverable
1												
2												
3												
4												
5												
6												
7												
8												
9												
10												
11												
12												
13												
14												
15												
16												
17												
18												
19												
20												
21												
22												
23												
24												
25												
26												
27												
28												
29												
30												

November Promotion Checklist

Pub Date	True Fans	Internal	Facebook	Instagram	Twitter	LinkedIn	SnapChat	Pinterest	YouTube	Appearances	Events	Publicity							
1																			
2																			
3																			
4																			
5																			
6																			
7																			
8																			
9																			
10																			
11																			
12																			
13																			
14																			
15																			
16																			
17																			
18																			
19																			
20																			
21																			
22																			
23																			
24																			
25																			
26																			
27																			
28																			
29																			
30																			

December

December

Sunday	Monday	Tuesday	Wednesday	Thursday	Friday	Saturday

Notes:

December Creation Checklist

Pub date	Scheduled	Title	Author	Keywords	Category	Tags	Image	Audio	Video	Links	SEO	Deliverable
1												
2												
3												
4												
5												
6												
7												
8												
9												
10												
11												
12												
13												
14												
15												
16												
17												
18												
19												
20												
21												
22												
23												
24												
25												
26												
27												
28												
29												
30												
31												

December Promotion Checklist

Pub Date	True Fans	Internal	Facebook	Instagram	Twitter	LinkedIn	SnapChat	Pinterest	YouTube	Appearances	Events	Publicity							
1																			
2																			
3																			
4																			
5																			
6																			
7																			
8																			
9																			
10																			
11																			
12																			
13																			
14																			
15																			
16																			
17																			
18																			
19																			
20																			
21																			
22																			
23																			
24																			
25																			
26																			
27																			
28																			
29																			
30																			
31																			